# Hope on a Rope

## Lifelines for Knuckleheads

## Bill S. Paige

"Unless otherwise noted, scriptures are taken from the ® NEW KING JAMES VERSION (NKJV) Copyright © 1982 by Thomas Nelson, Inc. Used by permission. All rights reserved.

First published in Greensboro, North Carolina

Printed in the United States of America          2017

Cover design: David Terry

ISBN: 978-0-692-88217-7

# Words of Praise for *"Hope on a Rope"*

*"Bill Paige is ALIVE! His Hope on a Rope takes us from his policing the streets of New York to his evangelizing in halls all over the world for Young Life. Jesus Christ changed Bill's life and then Bill went out into the world, with Jesus Christ, changing thousands of lives. Now, he writes it all down in stories that, like Bill, are ALIVE! Catch this rope!"*
Frederick Dale Bruner, author of Bible commentaries on the books of Matthew and John

*"This is a wonderful book and a true testimony of God's love and faithfulness. Bill is a gifted storyteller who has shared his faith in front of thousands. This book is inspiring, humorous and engaging. Through many challenges, Bill never lost hope – he clung to Jesus and only grew stronger in his faith. He encourages the reader to do the same."*
Pam Moore, Training Director of Young Life

*"I just completed reading Hope on a Rope and found it to be a thought-provoking yet inspirational book. Its format reads similar to a devotional as each chapter deals with real-life challenges faced in a human experience. Bill's personal testimony coupled with biblical scripture references and principles promotes self-reflection and the opportunity for change through a Hope in Jesus Christ."*
Barney Hilton Murray, Founder, Arizona Christian Men's Fellowship

*"Bill Paige uses his personal experiences to open the reader's mind to draw them to Christ and he uses the teachings of Jesus to show the reader how applying the scriptures can help them resolve the innermost questions about their life. He does a good job of showing the reader that the Bible is the means of deliverance and that the Scriptures really do apply to them."*
Senior Pastor Robert Colwell, Calvary Chapel Crenshaw, Los Angeles, CA

*"I've known Bill Paige for many years through our mutual involvement in Young Life. I thought I knew Bill well, yet many of the stories and insights he draws from his life in this book were new to me. Bill is an inspiring Christian, and the reader can see from this book where his inspiration comes from. God has walked with Bill along the way, making Himself known to Bill in unlikely and often surprising ways. What a guy – what a story!*
Jeff Pope, Minneapolis, MN

*"There are things that the Lord is trying to get out of our lives and He will exhaust Himself to do it," says Bill Paige in 'Hope on a Rope.' God's relentless, everlasting, loving pursuit for us is demonstrated in this testimonial from one of the most transparent books I have ever read. To the believer, Bill has a never ending journey of God's love, forgiveness and restoration in response to his many cycles, seasons and levels of decreasing so that Christ would be increased in Him. The book had me crying, cheering but most of all, feeling hopeful. It speaks volumes to every Christian, from babes sucking down the sincere milk of the 'Word of God' to the full grown (mature), capable of handling but on occasion, strangling on the 'Word' after being drawn away. 'Hope on a Rope' reminds us that God's sovereign love is ever present, seeking by way of the Holy Spirit, to transform a yielded son and daughter to the likeness of His dear Son, Jesus Christ, for true discipleship."*
Diedra Bynum, author of *"Jacob's Leah: In Her Shoes"*

*"For we are saved by hope"*
*(Romans 8:24a KJV)*

## This book is dedicated to:

- those in need of Hope;
- those who feel people have kicked them to the curb or in some cases, feel that they have kicked themselves;
- those who feel they have fallen so far that they believe there is no way back;
- those who feel they are at the end of their rope, hanging by a thread;
- those who go to bed nearly every night on a tear-stained pillow;
- those who are carrying the cruel scars of life and don't know what to do about those who inflicted them;
- those who have received hope and are encountering a host of people who need that same hope;
- those who have forgotten the hope that may have been extended to them at one time or another in their life;
- in other words, it is dedicated to those of us who are on a journey through this thing we call life. To all of us, who sooner or later are going to need Hope.

# Acknowledgements

First and foremost, these writings (the good, the bad and the ugly) were inspired by my Lord and Savior, Jesus Christ: without whose grace, mercy, and forgiveness, none of this would be possible.

The man who raised me, Shearl R. Paige. A decorated WWI veteran, he passed away at the ripe old age of 87. He died on Veteran's Day and I could not think of a better day. He received Jesus at the age of 83. Though not my biological father, he was my DADDY. I am eternally grateful for his love and care. He was a saving grace in my life.

My late wife Claudia, who passed away after a prolonged battle with chronic illness.

My sons, Randy and Lance, who have stood by my side through thick and thin.

My current wife, Pamela, who is God's demonstration of grace and love for my life.

Rev. Colleen Holby, who God used to help with my development as a man when we served together at Children's Village in Dobbs Ferry, NY.

The men and women who walked with me in my days of doing ministry in New Jersey and New York City, including Roy and Jesse Lisath, David Ireland, Helen Littleberry and Eric Butler. There are many others as well.

The wonderful men and women of Young Life, whom I served with for more than 21 years. Among them, I would give special recognition to Jim Eney and Paul Coty.

Denny Rydberg, who hired me at Young Life and had confidence in me to do the job he called me to do.

Ken Gire, whose books inspired me, taught me, encouraged me and even left me awestruck in regards to depth of the grace and love of our Savior. Along with him are a host of authors who the Lord used to help develop my life and ministry.

Finally, Jim and Mae Murray: I cherish their friendship, encouragement and support, especially the efforts of their team in reviewing and editing the manuscript from start to finish.

# Foreword

I have known Bill Paige for over 20 years. We first met at a Young Life camp in New York State and hit it off from the beginning. Over the years, we have worked closely together, become good friends, and shared the ups and downs of life together. In the midst of the good, bad, and ugly of life, we haven't lost our sense of humor nor our commitment to Jesus Christ.

One thing I learned about Bill early on is that he's a guy who tells the truth. And he continues to be a truth teller in this book. He tells the truth about God, the truth about the Bible, the truth about life, and the truth about himself. Anybody who has hung out with Bill or heard him speak knows that his conversation and message will be honest and vulnerable.

He brings this honesty, vulnerability, truth telling and faith to this book. He believes that all of us are "knuckleheads," and that as knuckleheads, we need help in how we follow Jesus. Being a knucklehead himself, Bill talks about the struggles he's had and how God has met him, made a huge difference in his life, and continued that refinement process. I've had the opportunity to watch God in action in the life of Bill, and I'm impressed by the faithfulness of God and the commitment of my friend Bill.

I recommend we all plunge into Bill's book and learn what he's learned. He came from a tough background and took on a difficult job as a policeman, and he does have stories to tell. But the greatest story is how the Lord pursued him and never let him go.

Denny Rydberg
President Emeritus
Young Life

# Introduction

I have been in the ministry for more than 30 years. I have had the opportunity to travel all over the United States and around the world. It has been an awesome blessing to see a multitude of people turn their lives over to Jesus. I have also found that a host of people are holding onto unresolved issues in their lives. These are folk both in the body of Christ and those who are not.

We cannot take our walk with the Lord for granted. Spiritual warfare is for real. We are warned that Satan is a worthy adversary. I believe the faith of every Christian is tested, perhaps on a daily basis (James 1:2). All too often, careless believers have found that out the hard way. This is a cautionary tale to everyone. The Bible exhorts us all in the scripture: *Wherefore let him that thinketh he standeth take heed lest he fall.* (I Corinthians 10:12 KJV).

The evidence is also found in the fulfillment of II Thessalonians 2:3: (KJV) *For that day shall not come, except there come a falling away first.* Many Christians are walking away from God's great gift of eternal life promised to every born again believer. Why? In many cases, it's because they have lost hope.

People are dying and time is short to get things right. So many people are carrying so much unforgiveness that it is unbelievable – and that is a sure pathway to spiritual defeat. Please know this: I have found myself from time to time listed among those with an assortment of issues.

Those issues can come in a multitude of ways. Trust me:
I have the battle scars to prove it!

After my 30 plus years in the ministry, 20 plus years in the
police department and the rest of the crazy life I have lived,
I have come to the following conclusion. There are two
kinds of people in the world: knuckleheads and people who
think they are not knuckleheads. That being said, I have at
times found myself to be the biggest one of all.

I would consider these kinds of people to be knuckleheads:

1. Someone who keeps making the same mistakes over
   and over.
2. Someone who keeps promising him or herself not to
   do this or that again, only to find themselves doing
   this or that again.
3. Someone who keeps saying to themselves, "What
   was I thinking?"
4. Someone who says to God (too many times), "I
   know I told you that I wouldn't do that again. But I
   did it again. Please forgive me again!"
5. Someone who has to seemingly learn everything the
   hard way.
6. Someone to whom the Lord says, "How's that
   working for you?"

If you do not fall into the definition, forgive me. I
release you from the list of folks who might. If this does
not apply to you now, maybe it applies to someone you
know.

But I truly believe there are very few people who have not
had a knucklehead moment, a knucklehead season, a
knucklehead experience, made a knucklehead decision or
experienced a knucklehead failure.

In my acknowledgements, I named folks who have helped me navigate the waters of life. During these years, I have encountered a host of other men and women who are trying to negotiate these waters as well. Some have done a great job and some, like me, have faltered along the path. This book is written as an encouragement to anyone who would dare sail with Jesus. I pray that it will give Hope and encouragement to all who read the pages herein. I pray that it will give clear pictures of God's grace and love. There are no shortages of lifelines!

Hope is a necessary survival tool and can only truly be found in Christ. I use scripture and my own life experiences to share tested and proven "lifelines" to those seeking relief, deliverance and victory. Hope, when resting on the foundation of faith, sustains believers and snatches them from the jaws of spiritual defeat. No matter what we face in life, we cannot afford to give up on Jesus.

The Apostle Paul raises a question in the book of Romans: *Who shall separate us from the love of Christ?* (Romans 8:35a KJV).

He answers in verses 38 and 39: *For I am persuaded, that neither death, nor life, nor angels, nor principalities, nor powers, nor things present, nor things to come, nor height, nor depth, nor any other creature shall be able to separate us from the love of God, which is in Christ Jesus our Lord.*

If we stand on the assurance of these words, our hope in Christ Jesus is secure from now to eternity!

# Table of Contents

## Chapter 1

# *Hope for the Journey*

*"Therefore, if anyone is in Christ, he is a new creation; old things are passed away; behold, all things have become new. Now all things are of God, who has reconciled us to Himself through Jesus Christ, and has given us the ministry of reconciliation."* I Corinthians 5:17-18

My life's journey began when I was born in 1947. I lived in a two-family home owned by my mother and father. I had two cousins who lived with me. One was a boy who was five years older than me. He was the brother that I never had. Mom and Dad never had any more kids, so he would suffice as that brother. I still consider him my brother to this day.

The other cousin was a girl who was 15 when I was born. I heard that she had a child somewhere along the line, but I never saw the child. She lived a pretty wild life. As a child, I saw things that children shouldn't see. But that was her life. I didn't think much of it then.

My mother never kissed or hugged me. I cannot remember her ever saying, "I love you."

While growing up in this atmosphere, I got into trouble all of the time. I would get some pretty serious beatings from time to time.

I remember dropping a piece of pie on the floor by accident.

"That day," my dad was putting the television antenna on the roof. The old antenna was in the driveway (these were the days before cable television). My mother beat me with that antenna. As I look back, I would call that somewhat of an overreaction. It was like being in the house with Zorro and not having a sword.

Personally, I don't have a problem with corporal punishment, but I do have issues with abuse. My beating did not kill me, but if it happened in today's society, someone would have been arrested.

There are a couple of other situations that I would consider abuse as well. I often think back to "that day" and wonder what that was all about. In the midst of all of this, my mom was a bookie for organized crime.

On the other hand, my father was a wonderful man. He worked for the post office as a courier. He never punished me or hit me physically. He was always there for me. And though I do not remember him ever saying, "I love you," I know that he did. I would later come to realize that he was one of God's saving graces in my life. He did his best to spoil me. I wonder if he was feeling sorry for me. I cannot ever remember being hit by my mom or anyone else while I was in his presence. Dad was the most wonderful man to walk the face of this earth, other than Jesus. I'm not sure what others thought about him, but I know how I felt.

As I grew up in this household, I would not have considered my life as unhappy, but I believe deep down inside, I was.

However, if anyone would have looked at my outward appearance, I don't think many people would have noticed. I seemed happy and content.

Mom had a couple of different places where we would stay. We had a house in the Bronx, a couple of apartments in Manhattan and a couple of places in New Jersey. As I write this, I wonder if we were in the Federal Witness program.

I was always getting in trouble in school. It was usually for some type of inappropriate behavior. Women teachers paid the price for having me as a student. I think I can relate this to my feelings towards my mother.

I was hanging out with some pretty wild guys. For the most part, they were good but some of their behavior began to turn criminal. I found myself gravitating in that direction.

In June, 1961, I had a "that day" moment. While living in New Jersey, I came home from school one day. I was 13-years-old and in the sixth grade. When I arrived, some of mom's friends were at the house. That was nothing new. People were always in the house, including the man I saw mom cheat with while dad worked in New York.

"That day," mom's friends told me that they had some bad news. They said mom had a massive heart attack and had passed away. I remember taking my dog for a walk. I think I walked for about an hour. I remember crying. I don't know why -- maybe glad, maybe sad.

When I got back home, my cousin had come home from school. He was 18 then. He saw that I had been crying. He asked me why. I told him because mom was dead.

He said, "So what. She's not your real mother. Your cousin Betty (who had been living in our house) is your real mother."

At first, I didn't believe him. Then, I found out that it was true. I cannot remember what I felt. My cousin's "bedside manner" was not the best, but his words were devastatingly true.

It was surreal on the day of the funeral. I remember that no one cried at the funeral home. However, I wept almost uncontrollably in the funeral car. Afterwards, for some reason, I had a fear that mom was not dead. It was like she was playing some kind of game and would reappear. I don't know why I had this fear.

All this time, my biological mother lived in our house and I thought she was my cousin. She lived a pretty wild lifestyle, some of it in my presence. I had been deceived (even if the deceivers meant well). I had been living a lie. I did not articulate that in my mind then, but it is crystal clear now.

After mom's death, things returned to normal. Dad, my cousin and I went back to living in the Bronx. I went to an all-boys high school. I was a pretty good athlete, playing football and baseball. My friends would not let me play basketball because I was too physically aggressive. I would do almost anything for attention.

But I think I was very discontented with what was taking place in my home. The abuse and lack of love from the person I thought was my mother -- but wasn't -- was becoming unbearable.

The love of my father was unquestionable.

He had never said a mean-spirited word to me nor had he ever abused me. He was always there for me. He loved me unconditionally. He did not express a lot of verbal affirmation, but his presence was more than enough. He never did one thing that would justify my leaving. But my mind was made up.

And on that day, I began planning the journey. It would begin six years later when I dropped out of school, began running the streets and did all that I was old enough to do. I joined the army to keep from going to jail.

While in the military, I got into quite a bit of trouble. A friend of mine told me I was "a soldier's dream but a sergeant's nightmare." I was always kicking against authority. Probably because one of the main authority figures in my life – my mom – abused her authority.

\*\*\*\*\*\*\*\*\*\*\*\*

Growing up in the Bronx, our house was directly in the glide path for LaGuardia Airport. These were the days of the DC6 and the Cosmopolitan airplanes (not jets). It seemed like the planes were close enough to hit with a rock.

Flights did not ascend as quickly as they do today. I was always intrigued as I watched them disappear over Manhattan. At night time, I would watch the skies. Planes would fly much higher and I would follow their lights as they blinked in the darkness. I wondered who was on those planes and where were they going.

More often than not, I wanted to be on one of those planes. I didn't care where it was going; I just wanted to be there. Often, it would bring tears to my eyes. Having grown up in a dysfunctional family, I wanted to escape and go on a journey: ANYWHERE!!

When that journey began, it would last for 14 years. It took a while to realize where home was. I would learn that I needed a new direction and a new destination. Only then did I come to my senses and say in essence, "I am going home."

It was December 26th, 1980. At 2:45 pm, Jesus Christ burst into my life. It was the day after Christmas that I received a belated birthday gift from the God of all creation. On "that day," I was watching the *700 Club* on television. Pat Robertson pointed at the screen. He asked, "Are you a sinner?" Then he asked, "Do you know Jesus?" I found myself talking to the television. I said, "Yes, I am a sinner." Then I said, "No, I don't know Jesus."

An 800 telephone number flashed on the screen. He said to call that number, and I did. I prayed with the man who answered the phone and I received Jesus as my Lord and Savior. My life has never been the same. "That day," like Peter, I got real. I came to Jesus, just like I was.

Immediately, He began a good work in me, just as His word promises (Philippians 1:6). I did not know *how much* work there was yet to do. But my journey had begun.

Little did I know that while I watched those planes flying over my home in the Bronx, I would later be on my way and my future would include flying about 100,000 miles in a year. Never could I imagine that eventually I would have flown over two million miles.

But that would be a long way off.

## "For We Are Saved By Hope"

## Chapter 2

# *Hope in Memories*

*"For I will be merciful to their unrighteousness, and their sins and their iniquities will I remember no more."* Hebrews 8:12  KJV

What an incredible verse and promise made by the Lord to us (more specifically, to me). This verse has always amazed me. Even as I read it today, it takes on a greater meaning. Grace is getting what we don't deserve. But mercy is not getting what we do deserve. At the beginning of the verse, the Lord lets the believer know that He has been and will be merciful. In other words, "Bill, I am not going to give you what you deserve." In spite of ALL that you have done, I am not going to hold it against you. Not only that, those things that you have done, I am going to completely forget about them.

Four definitions of "remember" are:
- to have or to keep an image or idea in your mind of (something or someone from the past);
- to think of (something or someone from the past) again;

- to cause (something) to come back into your mind;
- to keep (information) in your mind: to not forget (something).

It is amazing that the Lord has the ability to do that. The God who knows everything about anything or more importantly, anybody, has the ability to choose not to remember something.

That being said, it has baffled me why He has not given me the same ability. It is my memory of the deeds of my past that often cause the most drama for me. I am talking about my inability to shake free of some of the things that I have done -- both in Christ and out. There are things that I regret. There are things that are so embarrassing -- things that come to my mind seemingly out of nowhere. I can be having a nice day, listening to music, driving my car, spending time with someone that I care about, then something will get triggered and my day begins to spin downward.

I can see a scene in a movie that will remind me of something I did or said to someone. I can think of times that I have hurt those whom I said I loved the most. It sometimes creates a feeling of nausea or utter shame. I look in the rear view mirror of my life, hoping and praying that some of those things don't catch up with me. And yet the Lord has forgiven and forgotten those things as well. It seems too good to be true. But because the Lord said it, it is true.

I could be very wrong about this, but I think the reason that He does not allow me to forget, is so that I won't forget something else. I will never be able to forget the love, grace, mercy, and kindness that has been extended to me.

Maybe His thought is that I will never forget those things that I am utterly ashamed of because I will remember the horrible yet wonderful price that had to be paid for my sins. The sacrifice that Jesus made for me on the cross has to come into play in this wonderful yet sometimes painful scenario. Maybe it is something that God uses to keep me from returning to my vomit.

If I can focus in on the love that was demonstrated for me, listen to His indwelling Spirit, I can stay on track. Maybe in the looking back, I have focused on the wrong thing. What I should have focused on was a hill outside the walls of Jerusalem about 2,000 years ago. Maybe when the fires of temptation are burning hot, it is at those times I should focus on the Cross.

Amway used to have a teaching tape entitled, *Stinkin' Thinkin'*. I never went to work for Amway, but I know the reality of that title. I think of the Apostle Paul, who was more or less in the same boat until Jesus stepped into his life. He then became the champion of the faith, and the Lord did great things in his life as well as great things through his life. He was a man that wreaked havoc in the early church of Jesus Christ. This is how a servant of the Lord responded when the Lord told him to go and lay hands on Saul after he had been converted on the road to Damascus:

*"Then Ananias answered, Lord, I have heard by many of this man, how much evil he hath done to thy saints at Jerusalem. And here he hath authority from the chief priests to bind all that call on thy name."* (Acts 9:13-14 KJV)

There was fear of this man because of the damage that he was doing to the Church. The Bible goes on to say more about the reputation of Paul (then Saul of Tarsus) before he was saved. *"And straightway he preached Christ in the synagogues, that he is the Son of God. 21 But all that heard him were amazed, and said; Is not this he that destroyed them which called on this name in Jerusalem, and came hither for that intent, that he might bring them bound unto the chief priests?"* (Acts 9:20-21)

Paul gave this testimony in Acts 26:11: *"And I punished them (the believers in Jesus Christ) often in every synagogue, and compelled them to blaspheme; and being exceedingly mad against them, I persecuted them even unto strange cities."* The Message Translation uses even more descriptive language in Philippians 3:6 when it says: *"And lastly, Concerning zeal, persecuting the church; touching the righteousness which is in the law blameless."*

How did he deal with guilt once he came to the realization of the things that he done? How was he able to reconcile the damage and even the deaths he had caused to the children of God and the cause of Christ? How was he able to even get his mind around the grace and mercy of the Lord that had been extended to him? Did it ever cause him to have sleepless nights? Did it ever cause him to be like Peter on the night that he denied the Lord three times, only to hear the rooster crow, causing him to run away and weep bitterly?

I don't know, but I think that he had to go through times of anguish. I don't know anyone who has told me of a time soon after their conversion (especially someone who had committed what might be considered a horrible life of sin) who was not haunted by the deeds of their past.

When I preach and ask the audience, "Is there anyone who is haunted by the deeds of their past?" In most cases, the air is filled with hands and dropped heads.

And yet, this same Paul writes these words for our hearing, in Philippians:

> *"But what things were gain to me, those I counted loss for Christ." Yea doubtless, and I count all things but loss for the excellency of the knowledge of Christ Jesus my Lord: for whom I have suffered the loss of all things, and do count them but dung, that I may win Christ, And be found in him, not having mine own righteousness, which is of the law, but that which is through the faith of Christ, the righteousness which is of God by faith: That I may know him, and the power of his resurrection, and the fellowship of his sufferings, being made conformable unto his death; If by any means I might attain unto the resurrection of the dead. Not as though I had already attained, either were already perfect: but I follow after, if that I may apprehend that for which also I am apprehended of Christ Jesus. Brethren, I count not myself to have apprehended: but this one thing I do, forgetting those things which are behind, and reaching forth unto those things which are before."* (Philippians 3:7-13)

I know that he is the one who was inspired to write Romans 8, but how does the reality of verse 1 of that chapter become the reality in someone's life? I know the biblical answer is "by faith" and "trusting in the Lord," BUT how does it become a reality to me? I guess that Paul is also talking about more than looking back on his past life when he was a sinner.

But the sin part is what I want to concentrate on in my life. To forget it and simply appreciate the grace of God that has been extended to me. I remember when my mother was going to give me a beating. She would make me go out and get a switch. It would be a branch taken from a tree or bush. I was warned that I better not get one that breaks. Therefore, I was sent out to choose the weapon of my own torment (of sorts). This is just a random thought, but when God extends the Olive Branch, I wonder if I get it mixed up with the switch? I have far to go in regards to all of this. This is just the beginning.

We can always depend on God's unfailing love and His unfailing faithfulness to His children. If God can love a David and a Paul, he can surely love me. It is too good to be true. But the good thing about it: it is true!!

In my years of ministry, I have met a lot of people who felt that they could not be forgiven, but I cannot remember anyone who did not want to be forgiven. Whether you or I believe it or not, there is **no one** who cannot be forgiven. That is what makes God the God He is. As I stated earlier in the previous paragraph, "It's too good to be true, but it is true!!"

## Chapter 3

# *Hope in Temptation*

*"Blessed is the man who endures temptation; for when he has been approved, he will receive the crown of life which the Lord has promised to those who love Him. Let no one say when he is tempted, "I am tempted by God"; for God cannot be tempted by evil, nor does He Himself tempt anyone. But each one is tempted when he is drawn away by his own desires and enticed. Then, when desire has conceived, it gives birth to sin; and sin, when it is full-grown, brings forth death. Do not be deceived, my beloved brethren."* James 1:12-16

Have you ever been tempted?

Has an idea ever come into your mind that made all of the sense in the world at the time? Let me share such a moment in my life. It was early in my walk in the Lord. I was still on the police department and I was well acquainted with the "law."

God had done many great and marvelous things in my life. One of those things was the instant release from alcohol and substance abuse. I thought that I had arrived. And then it happened.

One day, I was driving on the Garden State Parkway in New Jersey. I was in Paramus, NJ by the Paramus Mall. On that day, I was struggling with my relationship with my wife. A thought came into my head. It was no ordinary thought. It seemingly came out of nowhere. It had a voice and that voice was as smooth as silk. It was not audible, but I could hear it as clearly as if it were. It said simply, "HE forgave David."

Instantly, the story of King David came into my mind. I loved reading about David. I loved the fact that he was a man after God's own heart. I remembered the night of his fall with Bathsheba. I remembered how he arose from his bed and walked out on the terrace. I remembered how he looked upon the woman that the New Scofield Reference translation of the Bible describes as, "pleasing to look upon." (II Samuel 11:2).

As a side note, I find it amazing that the writer of II Samuel, under the inspiration of the Holy Spirit, would describe her in that way. I love the reality of God. It was just one look that got the juices flowing in his flesh. That soon, it turned to lust and then "it happened." One thing led to another, which led to a host of other things.

However, on that night as I drove down the highway, I did not give all the "other" things too much thought. I was being tempted to commit adultery. I was offered a way out: to simply ask God's forgiveness with somewhat of an assurance that things would be OKAY.

Then, just as quickly, another voice entered into my head. This voice was not silky and smooth. As a matter of fact, it seemed kind of gruff. However, I knew the second voice was HIS voice.

HE simply (yet profoundly) said, "There must be a better reason not to commit adultery than because the Bible says, *"Do not commit adultery"* (Exodus 20:14). This statement flew in the face of the things I had been taught in my early walk with God.

Everyone knows the reason you don't commit adultery is because the Bible says, *"Thou shalt not commit adultery,"* right? I was perplexed. Why would the Lord tell me something that seemed contrary to what HE has written in HIS word? So, I went and did what God tells us to do in HIS word, *"Call to Me and I will answer and show you great and mighty things you did not know."* (Jeremiah 33:3) I said to Him, "Lord, what does that mean?"

This is what I believe the Lord showed me. The reason you don't commit adultery is that *"You love the Lord our God with all your heart, with all your soul, and with all your strength. The second is this: Love your neighbor as you do yourself."* (Mark 12:30-31)

These are words that come from the mouth of Jesus himself. I could see that God was saying, in essence, the reason not to commit adultery was because I loved HIM as described in that verse. The reason not to commit adultery was based on loving my neighbor as I did myself. In this case, my neighbor was my wife. He was also showing me that it was not about a rule of what not to do, but about the principles of what to do. It was not about rules; it was about love.

That day, I learned that when I am told not to do something, there is a strong tendency to do exactly the opposite. When inspired to do something with the right motivation, it is so much easier to accomplish.

There can be no greater motivation than LOVE. Jesus is Love. Simply put, Love God and Love people. Nothing else matters. If I were to just love God and my neighbors, all the bases would be covered. Jesus did not only go about not committing sin. Not only did Jesus go about not committing sin, but He also went about doing good. And because HE always did good, HE never committed sin. The motivation of all His actions and words were HIS love for HIS father and HIS love for the people HE came to serve.

I learned some valuable lessons on the highway that day. I learned of the faithfulness of God. HE does not want us to fail. We don't have to fail. The temptations that we go through are common to everyone. HE promised that HE would not allow us to be tempted above what we are able to bear. He would always provide a way of escape (I Corinthians 10:13).

He is an ever present help in a time of trouble and we can always run to HIM (Psalm 46:1). If you read the entire story about King David's fall, you will see that there are serious consequences for not doing life God's way. "What is God's way?" you might ask. Spike Lee said, "Do the right thing." Jesus would say, "Do the Loving thing!"

I wish I would have applied that principle to other situations that occurred in my walk with Christ. That day, I learned the easy way; at other times, it didn't go that smoothly. But those are "Memories" that long since have been taken care of by the Lord.

# Chapter 4

# *Hope in Anger*

*"Therefore, putting away lying, let each one of you speak truth with his neighbor, for we are members one of another. Be angry and do not sin."* Ephesians 4:25-26

Have you ever said something in a moment of being upset that as soon as you said it, you knew you shouldn't have? Have you ever done something in a moment of anger that felt good when you did it but later regretted that you went there? Or, have you ever been upset with someone who did not know that you were upset with them? As soon as they come into your presence, you start thinking all kinds of evil things in your heart. What is that all about? At times, I don't know. But I do know this: "What's in the well will come up in the bucket." If there are unresolved issues in our lives, they will surface sooner or later.

It was a cold winter evening. I was working the 5 pm to 1 am tour. I was a detective and working alone. There was nothing going on and the evening had been relatively quiet. I rode with the windows down and the heat in the vehicle was blasting. I liked the cold air on my face and the warmth on the rest of my body. In fact, it was quite warm.

As can happen at any time, the radio dispatcher sent two marked vehicles to what was called a "10-29." It was a fight in progress at a racquetball facility located in a corporate park. I had never heard of a fight at this particular location. I was close enough and decided to back up the responding vehicles. It was not my responsibility but I craved the excitement. I had a reputation for being a crazy driver, and I liked it. So keeping in line with the reputation, I drove like an idiot to get there (of course, I did not look at it that way then).

Surprisingly enough, I was the first car on the scene. There was a small crowd gathered around two men who were arguing. The more aggressive of the two men was being held back by some of the people in the crowd. Usually in a fight, one of the parties is always happy to see the police arrive (the one who is losing the fight)!! I was in plain clothes, so I identified myself as a police officer and stepped between the two men.

I paid more attention to the man who seemed the most volatile. I tried to find out what had happened. The other man said his "friend" was upset because he had beaten him in racquetball. To add to the issue, his friend had been drinking. At this, his friend became more frenzied and began screaming curses and threats.

At that point, all of his anger became directed at me. I had been a Christian for only a week. I was known to have had a pretty bad temper, and I could feel it beginning to rise. It was my first confrontation in my newly found faith. I loved Jesus dearly and did not want to do anything that would upset Him. The cursing continued, and I could literally feel the curse words.

I look back on it now and feel that they were fiery darts being hurled at me. I literally began to growl under my breath and my anger began to kick in. No matter what I said or how calmly I said it, the man would not be dissuaded. He threatened to kill his friend, at which point, I informed him that was not going to happen. Then, he threatened to kill me. I felt myself reaching the breaking point.

Then, unexpectedly the man stepped towards me, reached up and pinched my cheek and told me that I was "sweet." At that point, I felt all control go out the window. There is no exaggeration in what I am about to say. I made up my mind to grasp him by the head, lean in and bite the nose off of his face!

This course of action made complete sense to me at the time. However, I now know that was not the prompting of the Holy Spirit. As my plan of action went into effect, a strange thing happened. I can't really explain it. My hand went into my mouth and I clamped down across my four fingers and screamed. I then knew that I needed to distance myself from this man or I was going to do something that "we" would regret.

When I turned to move away, there were five police officers standing there. I had never heard them arrive at the scene. One of the officers (a patrolman at that time) and one of my closest friends in the department said, "Now we know you are a Christian."

Up until that time, none of my friends, colleagues, or family members really believed that Jesus had come into my life. However, as I look back on that incident, things would have gone quite differently had they happened eight days prior.

You might not understand, but it is truly a testament of what God can do in someone's life. It is the reality of the verse that says, *If anyone is in Christ, they become a new creation. The old is gone and the new has come.* (II Corinthians 5:17) The police officers who knew who I was and how I was before Jesus came into my life had a ringside seat to see what the Lord can do! I turned the situation over to them and resumed my duties for the evening.

That night stands out in my mind for two reasons. The first is that you never know who is watching you after you proclaim that Jesus is the Lord of your life. These were men who were very much acquainted with the "Old Bill," namely the drinker, the brawler, the knucklehead. They could not grasp that my life had been so radically changed by Jesus.

The second reason is I wondered why I had become so enraged. I now use an expression, "What is in the well will come up in the bucket." I know now (but not then) that there were unresolved issues of anger deep down on the inside. Those issues were simmering just below the surface and it did not take much to bring them to light. Unfortunately, the instant delivery from alcohol and substance abuse had fooled me into thinking that I "had arrived." Little did I know that this was just the beginning of the journey.

I found that the Lord is true to His Word. He promises that He will never allow us to be tempted by greater circumstances than we can handle. He further promises that with those temptations, He will provide the way of escape (I Corinthians 10:13). That night, I was allowed to bite my hand rather than the nose on that man's face. However, those issues needed to be dealt with. He also made a promise in that regard as well when His word says, *He that has begun a good work in you will perform it until the day of Jesus Christ.* (Philippians 1:6)

In the upcoming chapters, we will look at how God gives us hope in our anger. I had no idea of just how broken I was when I came to Jesus as I was. I had no idea of how faithful He is to His promises to us.

At the time of this writing, when NYC Police Officers were in trouble, they would call for help on the radio with a signal called "10-13." If you are willing, you can search the scriptures and find some pretty amazing scriptures involving "10-13" calls where the Lord comes to the rescue.

## "For We Are Saved By Hope"

# Chapter 5

# *Hope in Forgiveness*

*"Then Peter came to Him and said, 'Lord, how often shall my brother sin against me, and I forgive him? Up to seven times?' Jesus said to him, 'I do not say to you, up to seven times, but up to seventy times seven. Therefore the kingdom of heaven is like a certain king who wanted to settle accounts with his servants. And when he had begun to settle accounts, one was brought to him who owed him ten thousand talents. But as he was not able to pay, his master commanded that he be sold, with his wife and children and all that he had, and that payment be made.*
*35 So my heavenly Father also will do to you if each of you, from his heart, does not forgive his brother his trespasses.'"* Matthew 18:21-22, 35

It seems to me that Peter had an issue with someone. I don't think this was a hypothetical question. Maybe he had every right to be angry. Maybe he had forgiven that person seven times. He goes to Jesus to get crystal clear clarity on the subject.

I often think, "Don't ask questions you don't really want to know the answers to," or better still, "Don't ask questions if you are unwilling to deal with the truth of the answers to those questions."

I am not saying that is the way that Peter felt. I only know that there have been times that I have gone to the Lord and asked questions and not gotten the answer that I wanted. The reason can be found in Isaiah 55 when the Lord says, *"For My thoughts are not your thoughts, nor your ways My ways, says the Lord. For as the heavens are higher than the earth, so are My ways higher than your ways, and My thoughts than your thoughts."* (Isaiah 55:8-9)

I heard an expression that said, "The only stupid question is the question that you don't ask." But what happens when you ask the question, get the right answer and don't follow it through?

\*\*\*\*\*\*\*\*\*\*\*\*

In May of 2013, I had accepted two speaking opportunities in Uganda, Africa. One was with Young Life, and the other in partnership with a church from Long Island, NY. At that time, I was traveling a lot and was on the road for more than 200 days a year. The ministry seemed to be quite fruitful.

This was my second trip to Africa. I was excited about going. The first engagement was with the staff and volunteers who were serving Young Life in Africa. There were well over 100 people in attendance. The conference lasted four days.

While in Africa, you have to be careful about food and water. As a matter of fact, all food should be cooked and no water consumed unless it is bottled. I was very careful to follow the rules. But on the last day of the conference, I woke up early in the morning. I washed up and brushed my teeth. I forgot the water rule and ran my toothbrush under the faucet. I did not think much of it. I left the conference pleased with what I believed the Lord had done in our lives.

I traveled to Entebbe and arrived at the hostel where I would be staying. I was tired and I went to bed early. I awoke in the middle of the night in a pool of feces. This is going to sound gross, but it felt comfortable: the room was chilly yet the mess was warm. At first, I did not want to get up.

This may have been because I was tired. I thought I heard the Lord say, "You like laying in your filth, don't you?" I felt that it was a reminder of times when I was unwilling to change a course of behavior that I know was not pleasing to Him. (I believe I got a stomach virus from the only time I could think of where I violated that "water rule.") The stomach virus cleared up in a couple of days. I was able to speak at the youth conference in Entebbe. It was now time to return to the States.

I boarded a flight on that Saturday. I had made arrangements to be home for Mother's Day that Sunday. I fly about 100,000 miles a year. I was pretty exhausted. I was falling asleep shortly after takeoff. I think the flight was just getting up to 20,000 feet, when I heard two loud explosions. My first thought was, "I never heard a noise like that before."

The plane started descending. There was a scurry among the flight attendants. They were all white with what seemed to be few if any tanning pigments. However, their faces were beet red. I knew that they were rattled though their composure was intact. I said to the Lord, "Jesus, am I coming to see you today?"

When the engine on your plane blows up, God has a captive audience! You begin praying in the King James English. Unfortunately, I live in a state of denial regarding plane crashes.

I look around and say to myself, "It is a shame that all of these people have to die." I always feel that I am going to be the one who will survive. (However, this was Africa. I felt that I would live through the crash only to be eaten by some wild animal in the jungle.) I am glad that I never got a chance to put this thinking to the test.

The pilot did a skillful job in getting the plane back to the airport in Entebbe. He was able to land the plane with the one engine that did not have trouble.

There was no panic in the plane. However, when the engine blew up, the power on the television screens went out as well. The flight map was on and we were headed to Belgium. When it came back on, we were headed back to Entebbe. This caused a stir among the passengers. I am always amazed at something like this. What are people thinking? "Let's ignore the explosion and go the remaining 5,000 miles on one engine." Personally, I was not in that much of a hurry.

We landed and arrangements were made for us to go out on different airlines. I got out a day later. I did not make it home for Mother's Day, but I made it home (hence the writing of this story). Here is an official report of the incident according to *The Aviation Herald*:

*The Aviation Herald*
*Last Update: Sunday, May 26th 2013*
*14:01Z13525 Articles available Events from*
*Jun 19th 1999 to May 25th 2013*
*www.avherald.com*
*Incidents and News in Aviation*
*Incident: Brussels A332 at Entebbe on May 12th 2013, engine shut down in flight*

*By Simon Hradecky, created Thursday, May 16th 2013 21:07Z, last updated Thursday, May 16th 2013 21:09ZA Brussels Airlines Airbus A330-200, registration OO-SFY performing flight SN-465 from Entebbe (Uganda) to Brussels (Belgium), was climbing out of Entebbe about 20 minutes into the flight when the right hand engine (PW4168) emitted a series of bangs and streaks of flames (usually indicative of engine compressor stalls or surges) prompting the crew to shut the engine down and return to Entebbe for a safe landing about 40 minutes after departure. The airline confirmed the aircraft returned to Entebbe due to engine compressor stalls. The engine is to be replaced, the incident aircraft is currently still in Entebbe (standing May 16th 21:00Z) causing disruptions to the flight schedule of Brussels Airlines.*

After I returned home, I had to leave again to speak at a Men's Conference in British Columbia. When I left home, everything seemed to be okay with my health. However, when I arrived at the camp, I took my bags up a flight of stairs and noticed that I was completely out of breath. This had never happened to me before. I am not in the best of shape, but I had not had a problem with walking up stairs. I did not give it too much notice but felt that I needed to see a doctor when I got back home.

The following Monday, I went to see my family physician. He checked me out and gave me an EKG. He said, with great concern in his voice, "You need to see a cardiologist right away."

An appointment was made that day. Upon the completion of his examination, it was determined that I had Cardiac Heart Failure. On the first visit, he began discussing the possibility of the need for a heart transplant. Of course, I was not interested in getting a heart transplant. I suggested maybe we should start with an aspirin. However, again, God had my attention.

At the same time, my wife Claudia began to develop issues with her liver. After 16 years of health problems, her liver began to deteriorate. She had to be hospitalized on several occasions. I began having to cancel speaking engagements.

Finally, she had a liver transplant. Over the years, I watched her struggle through the complications before and after that surgery. I did not want any part of a transplant if it could be avoided. I sent out an email to all my prayer partners and asked them to pray that the Lord would do something miraculous.

I started riding my bike. At first, it was strenuous. However, I got up to 14 miles before my next visit with the cardiologist. It was then decided that I would not need a transplant. God was faithful. It has since been decided that this issue will be chronic but treatable with medicine. I will have to take pills for the rest of my life, but I keep the same heart that I came into this world with!! Well, at least to some capacity.

This is something that had never happened before. During this time, the Lord began to deal with the issues of my spiritual heart. He began to show me myself in the scriptures.

The verse that He took me to is in the book of Revelation in the second chapter. Here is what it says:

*"To the angel of the church in Ephesus, write: ' These are the words of him who holds the seven starts in his right hand and walks among the seven golden lampstands: I you're your deeds, your hard work and your perseverance. I know that you cannot tolerate wicked men, that you have tested those who claim to be apostles but are not, and have found them false. You have persevered and have endured hardships for my name, and have not grown weary. Yet I hold this against you: You have forsaken your first love.'"* (Revelation 2:1-4 NIV)

In verse 4, He says to the church in Ephesus that it has left its first love. In another translation, it says they do not love as they did at first. As I write this, I can see that looking at it both ways would be appropriate. God was showing me that He was no longer my first Love, Him. Nor did I love Him in the way that I used to. Nor did I love Claudia the way that I used to.

This is what it began to look like. Because of all the speaking engagements that I was getting, I was starting to like what I did more than who I was doing it for. Ministry was quickly becoming an idol to me. I was beginning to enjoy the accolades and strokes that came with being successful.

Success can become the biggest trap. You think that because you are doing well and people are giving you all sorts of strokes (which feed directly into your ego), that God is pleased.

You watch folks be blessed by what you say. You see people respond to the grace of God. No one is complaining, at least not to your face.

You do not realize that you are on a very slippery slope that is leading you away from the Lord. You begin to like the benefits that come with being a Frequent Flyer. You slowly drift into an attitude of entitlement. In other words, you are completely stuck on yourself. I thank God that He is a jealous God.

When He says He loves us, He really means it. He will do whatever He has to and whenever He has to, to get the point across.

*************

I married my high school sweetheart, Claudia, while I was in the military. This happened just before being sent to Korea. When I got married, I brought all of my baggage with me. Claudia never really knew what she was getting herself into. Unfortunately, she was the victim of a lot of that baggage. I got out of the military in late 1969 and became a police officer in May of 1970.

Like Claudia, the police department didn't know what it was getting into when they hired me. And like my marriage, I brought all of my baggage with me. They gave me a badge and a gun: a lot of authority but no power. As a result, I abused the authority.

Like in the military, I was a police officer who was always getting in trouble. However, in spite of all that, I made detective early. And I was also on the SWAT team.

But I was living a dual life, both at home and on the department. I was a hypocrite in every sense of the word. I was a liar, a cheat, abusive and a drunk. You name it, I was doing it.

\*\*\*\*\*\*\*\*\*\*\*\*

I stayed on the police department for 10 more years after I was converted to Christ, retiring in 1990. It was 20 exciting years that I wouldn't trade for anything. However, in 1986, I found myself working as the associate chaplain at a facility called Children's Village in Dobbs Ferry, NY. It was a residential treatment center for emotionally disturbed boys. The facility had 300 young residents. The chaplain was a woman who had been on the Young Life staff for 17 years before getting married and beginning her work at Children's Village (CV).

I didn't know that when I took the job, it was more for my benefit than for the benefit of the kids. I had an awesome time building relationships with those boys. I could relate to them and they could relate to me. I became a licensed trainer for staff. I taught a program called Therapeutic Crisis Intervention. The program showed how to assist kids who began acting out violently and how to restore them to the program. I loved teaching that course.

As a matter of fact, the Lord allowed me to spiritualize the program. Now, I use it in teaching how the Lord gets us through some of the dark periods of our lives. I would have loved to have been able to teach the program to the kids. They needed to learn how to deal with the staffers who were acting out!

The biggest lesson I learned in the 14 years I was at the Village is this: DON'T DO ANY MORE DAMAGE!! Those kids were damaged because of the dysfunctional homes they had been exposed to. They had never learned how to effectively and rationally deal with the crises that were in their lives. If the truth be told, neither had I.

As stated, because of the abuse of authority in my life, I was kicking against authority (especially from women). That being said, I find it amazing that the Lord would give me a woman for a boss. I was the associate chaplain and she was the chaplain. According to the word of God, I am instructed to obey those in authority (Hebrews 13:7). In my "bible," it says, "Unless it is a woman." (I wrote that in there. But it has no validity before the Lord whatsoever).

As I worked at CV, I was continually clashing with my supervisor. However, she had no idea of the baggage that I was carrying due to the abuse, betrayal and rejection I received as a child. How could she have? I was unaware of it myself. I had never looked back at it or talked about it. She was getting sick and tired of my not-so-passive aggression.

I had broken up many fights while I was at CV. Because of my police background, I was used to doing just that. I had learned well some more techniques to use through the Therapeutic Crisis program that I taught. Most of the fights at the Village were the results of kids taunting each other about their family relations – especially each other's mothers. It's amazing what things can be expressed through words.

"Sticks and stones may break my bones, but words will NEVER hurt me" is one of the biggest lies ever told.

Words can do far more damage than sticks and stones. And the wounds last a lot longer as well.

One day, my boss had gotten fed up with my resistance to her authority. On "that day," she confronted me. She put her hand on her hip and with eyes afire, she looked at me and asked, "What kind of a mother did you come from?"

Her words penetrated a part of me that had never been touched before (at least not as far as I knew). I was stunned and upset, yet I didn't know why. One thing I did know. I needed to find an answer to that question (if not for her sake, definitely my own). At this point in my life, my tongue was a very effective weapon. I had used it many times to reduce people to tears. I chose not to do this "that day." Instead, I turned and walked away. I got in my car and drove. I had no particular destination in mind. I rolled that question over and over in my head. The answer came.

I had two mothers who messed up my life. They were both dead: mom died when I was 13, and Betty (my real mother) died when I was 20. They were dead, and I was still angry at both of them. Mom, because of the abuse and lack of love. Betty, because of the rejection (she tried to have me aborted at birth), betrayal and deceit.

There were many more things I could add to the list, but that is unnecessary right now. I cannot explain what happened next. I heard myself say these words, "Mommy, wherever you are, I forgive you. Betty, wherever you are, I forgive you. Father, I ask you to forgive me for what I have allowed that caused me not to do this before."

Something else happened that I cannot fully explain. I literally felt some type of weight come off of me.

I never knew I was carrying that weight. I knew in my heart of heart that something incredible had taken place. I was set free from the anger, hatred, resentment and bitterness I never knew I had. It was utterly incredible. I went back to the Village and told my boss what had happened. We celebrated, to some degree. I know that from "that day," forth, my life has never been the same. It was one of the most transformative days of my Christian life. God had proven Himself great again!

There were many lessons to be learned from all of this. The first thing is that neither Mommy nor Betty deserved my forgiveness. Most of all, I did not deserve the forgiveness of God either. That is why He has given us His word, which says in the Phillips' Translation: *Let there be no more resentment, no more anger or temper, no more violent self-assertiveness, no more slander and no more malicious remarks, Be kind to each other, be understanding. Be as ready to forgive others as God for Christ's sake has forgiven you.* (Ephesians 4:31-32)

Take a look at that last verse. The reason we forgive has very little to do with what has been done to us. To me, forgiveness is all about what has been done **for** us. God has forgiven us for all of our sin. For that to happen, Jesus had to pay the price for our sin. The price was His life. Remember: *But God demonstrates His own love toward us, in that while we were still sinners, Christ died for us.* (Romans 5:8)

Simply put, God might say, "I forgave you for ALL your sin (and it cost my Son His life). After all I have done for you, do this little thing for me. Forgive them."

I know that it doesn't seem like a little to us, but in comparison to what it cost Jesus, it is. What took place "that day," I would call the great exchange. I exchanged all those negative emotions and the behavior that accompanied them for the peace of God that guards my heart and mind. I received the joy of the Lord, which is my strength, and new revelation about the grace of God.

Lastly, I know some might read this and say, "Bill, you don't understand." Others might say, "You don't know what they did to me." Still another might say, "I will never forgive them."

The Bible tells us, *For we do not have a High Priest who cannot sympathize with our weaknesses but was in all points tempted as we are, yet without sin.* (Hebrews 4:15)

There is nothing that we go through that Jesus is not acquainted with (he experienced). He empathizes with the hurt and pain because He has been there. Whatever has been done to us pales in comparison to what they did to Jesus. The word of God reminds us: *looking unto Jesus, the author and finisher of our faith, who for the joy that was set before Him endured the cross, despising the shame and has sat down at the right hand of the throne of God. For consider Him who endured such hostility from sinners against Himself, lest you become weary and discouraged in your souls.* (Hebrews 12:2-3)

The Lord reminds us of the importance of forgiveness when He says: *For if you forgive men their trespasses, your heavenly Father will also forgive you. But if you do not forgive men their trespasses, neither will you Father forgive your trespasses.* (Matthew 6:14-15)

In and of itself, this should make us willing to forgive someone else their sins against us. If your life is anything like mine, I spend quite a bit of time asking God to forgive me for things. I would not want to put something in the way of receiving that forgiveness.

It is all a choice. God has not only given us the edict to forgive but the ability to accomplish that forgiveness. Remember, Jesus said, *Without me, you can do nothing.* (John 15:5)

I have shared these things hoping that "this day" might turn into a "that day" for you to remember.

***********

He did that for me during the summer of 2013. I had several speaking engagements during that summer. Claudia's health was not improving. I had always made arrangements for her to be well taken care of. This time, it was going to be different. I was going to be the caretaker. It seemed like one day the Lord said to me, "You are going to take care of her. AND YOU NEED TO BE OK WITH THAT!"

He was getting to the bottom of issues in my life. The Bible says, *If a man says, I love God, and hates his brother, he is a liar: for he that loves not his brother whom he hath seen, how can he love God whom he hath not seen? And this commandment have we from him, That he who loves God loves his brother also.* (I John 4:20-21)

God was showing me something. Claudia and I were married for over 45 years when all of this was happening. A lot had happened between us; the good, the bad, and the ugly.

Unfortunately, our marriage had turned into more of a brother sister relationship rather than a husband and wife relationship. I never could have imagined how that would turn out.

He also showed me that I was going to stay home. I would cook, wash clothes, take out the garbage, shop, give Claudia her medicines and take her to numerous doctor appointments and hospital visits. It turned out to be a great blessing. Slowly but surely, I began to fall in love with her again. By serving her, I believe our intimacy began to increase.

It broke my heart to watch her struggle. She was a real trooper. It became evident that the possibility of another transplant was just over the horizon. There were times that my heart broke for her. Her liver levels were not yet high enough for her to get a transplant. Her lungs had to be tapped of fluids on four or five different occasions. She never complained. She demonstrated a type of courage that can only come through the grace of God.

In September of that year, we had a very important conversation. I had always felt that Claudia had not forgiven me for the adultery that I had committed before we were saved. She always confessed that she did, but I felt she hadn't. She always told me that I had not forgiven myself. She was absolutely right. Yet, I still felt that I was right about her unforgiveness. Again, we left the conversation there, though I felt the situation was still unresolved.

During this period of time, the Lord was showing me that who Claudia and I were to Him was far more important than anything we could have done for Him. He loved us, and He wanted us to love Him and love each other.

Marriage is very tricky. You have to always keep your hand on the pulse. If you are not careful, you can begin to live your lives as brother and sister rather than husband and wife.

One day, the Lord showed me this picture. He said, "You and Claudia are like railroad tracks. Your lives are parallel and you are going in the same direction, but you are going there separately. He said, "I want to turn those railroad tracks into a monorail, so you can go there together." I was able to see that through years of pain and hurt (both in Christ and out), we had allowed ourselves to drift apart. He was in the process of healing us.

Evidences of this drifting would manifest itself through the years. It was a continual nagging that plagued both of us. It would never completely go away. It is not important for me to discuss those in detail. In October, Claudia and I were watching television on our living room couch. I felt the Lord was nudging me to re-address the issue of forgiveness.

I asked her permission to talk about something that would be kind of hard to discuss. With a small look from her (which I interpreted, "Here we go again.") I said to her, "Claudia, I believe that you have not forgiven me for the adultery that I committed against you."

She assured me that she had. I insisted (in a very gentle way) that I believed that she had not. At this time, I want you to know that it is very difficult (though not impossible) to be part of the healing process when you were the one who created the wounds (especially if the issue has not been resolved).

When we had talked about this in the past, she would insist that she had forgiven me and the conversation would come to an end. This time it would be different. I maintained my stance that I felt the issue was unresolved. I felt the Lord leading me to do this as well.

Before I go any further, if it was not the Lord's leading, there was a chance that I could reopen a wound and inflict some more damage. I cannot emphasize enough, the importance of *knowing* it's the Lord and *thinking* it's the Lord. I felt very strongly that it was the Lord, so I proceeded. (However, looking back over the years that I have followed Jesus, I am sure of other times that I thought it was and the Lord, and it wasn't).

This time, I took the conversation in a different direction. I asked her this question: "Tell me what it looked like when you forgave me? What was your conversation with the Lord?" I felt that I needed to be very careful about my tone of voice. I needed to be inquisitive, rather than judgmental.

This was her response: "I told the Lord that He was going to have to take this." I thought about what she said. The Bible tells us that we can cast all of our care upon him because He cares for us (1 Peter 5:7). I felt that she was right in doing that. However, I felt that what she did was not forgiveness. I believe that we cannot ask the Lord to do for us, the things He has asked us to do. I shared those thoughts with her and she was in full agreement.

We talked some more. We came to a point in our conversation where she realized that she had not truly forgiven me. That day, we prayed out loud. She chose to forgive me for the adultery that I had committed.

We also chose to forgive each other for any other sins that we had committed against each other and we forgave where we felt that we had been sinned against. We prayed this prayer out loud. It was utterly awesome. WE resigned ourselves to completely let go of the past and never bring up anything that we had placed under the blood of Jesus that day.

Unfortunately, about a week later, I broke that rule. Claudia was quick (way too quick as far as I am concerned) to point that out to me. I confessed my wrong, and just as quickly, she forgave me. From that point on, we never went back to the past again. We also asked the Lord to manifest the healing that comes with forgiveness as well. When Jesus said, *Without me you can do nothing.* (John 15:5), He was not playing. He gives us the ability to make a choice, and then He does the rest.

That day, the slate was wiped clean. We were freely able to move forward. Little did I know that three months later, Claudia would be taken Home by Jesus. The last year of her life was one of the best years if not the best year of our marriage. Though we both struggled through difficult health issues, we did it together.

We prayed a prayer together and asked God to manifest the ability for that forgiveness to become a reality. She was willing to do that although I did not deserve it. I did not deserve it as much as either of us deserved the forgiveness of the Lord. Yet, He gave it to us. I did not realize that three months later, Claudia would find herself in the bosom of Jesus as He graciously brought her Home. In His amazing grace, I believed He reconciled us to one another.

When she went home to be with Him, the slate was clean regarding the issue of forgiveness.

Well, we see and hear what Jesus said to Peter. Are we willing to do what the Lord prescribes? It might be hard, but it is not impossible. Remember, we can do all things through Christ who gives us the strength. (Philippians 4:13) I don't know what Peter did with what Jesus told him. The question is: what are we going to do with what He tells us? God is the same yesterday, today and forever! His word does not change. We are told not to be just hearers of God's word, but doers.

He has made an investment in your life through the precious blood of His Son Jesus who died on the cross. He has placed His Spirit within you. He is not about to turn His back on that type of investment. He allows you to drift on the river of no return. Because of His love, He does not allow you to go over the falls. He has a way of reaching out to His children. He is not angry though He is grieved.

He is madly in love with us and realizes that what is happening will end in ruin. He only wants the best for His children. He wants better for us more than we could ever want for ourselves. His word says, *"I will withhold no good thing from you."* (Psalm 84:11) In His desire to give us all good things, He will often keep us from getting the things that can lead to our downfall or destruction.

God was not finished with the issues of forgiveness yet. Claudia passed away in January, 2014. My two sons and I went to the hospital after we decided to sign a do-not-resuscitate order. Claudia's health had greatly deteriorated.

She needed another liver transplant, but the operation would have killed her.

That day, we spoke with the doctors and they delicately and graciously explained the procedure. We asked the doctors how much more time she would have with us. They felt that she would probably live another 10 days or so.

She died within an hour.

My older son and I were in the hallway talking with Claudia's mother. My younger son went into the room where Claudia was resting. It was about the 57th minute of that hour. Claudia was in a state of delirium because of the toxins in her system.

He came out of the room and called for my older son and I to come into the room. He felt that she was getting ready to pass. By this time, Claudia's mother had left. The three of us stood by the bed as Claudia breathed her last breath and went into the arms of Jesus.

I cannot explain to you what happened next, but the room was suddenly filled with the joy of the Lord. All three of us sensed it. We had a peace that defied imagination.

We notified the staff and they made the official pronouncement. Then, our younger son Lance told us what had happened while he was in the room alone before Claudia passed away. He said that he stood beside the bed and said something to the effect of, "Mommy, I want you to forgive me for the anger, resentment and bitterness that I have held against you since I was a little boy."

He said that Claudia seemingly came out of the state of delirium and said, "I love you."

She closed her eyes and went to be with Jesus. The last words he heard his mother say was, "I love you."

Some of the last words she heard him say were, "Forgive me."

What an incredible God we serve. He covers all the bases and He does everything well. Before Claudia left for her new home in glory, the Lord allowed the slates to be wiped clean. Just like He does when we confess our sin to Him, He is faithful and just to forgive us and cleanse us from all unrighteousness. (I John 1:9)

I have found over the years that forgiveness is not only for the one who is forgiven, but it is also for the one who is the forgiver. I have also found that forgiveness has nothing to do with what has been done to you. It is about what has been done for you. *And be ye kind one to another, tenderhearted, forgiving one another, even as God for Christ's sake hath forgiven you.* (Ephesians 4:32).

The reason to forgive is because of what Jesus Christ did at the cross in order for all of us to be forgiven. No matter how moral we might be, Jesus still had to die for us.

To me, that verse says, the reason to forgive is simply because God has forgiven you. It has nothing to do with what has been done to you, it is all about what has been done for you. God through His mercy and grace has chosen to forgive us of ALL of our sin.

As a result, He asks us to forgive others for the sins they commit against us (which are far less than the number of sins we have committed against Him). This should be a tremendous blessing for the believer. Earlier, I mentioned that it is hard to be the healer when you have been the one who caused the wound. It is like hitting someone in the head with a hard object and asking to put ice on it for them. Duh!

I choose to belabor this subject because I see so much of it in the Church and in the World. You choose to forgive the offender based on the fact that God has forgiven you. It does not minimize the hurt and suffering you have encountered. It does not mean it was okay for you to be hurt. It does not mean that the offender will get off free. It simply means that you are choosing to forgive and placing the issue at the feet of Jesus. He is aware and is able to handle the situation in any way He sees fit. You then are able to move on with your life. Though the pain of the wound may still be there, God is able to bring about total healing. There is an expression, TIME HEALS ALL WOUNDS. I beg to differ. Time doesn't heal anything. The Bible says, *"I am the Lord who heals you."* (Exodus 15:26) God uses time, but ultimately, HE IS THE HEALER.

On that day, Claudia chose to forgive me. In God's amazing grace, I believed He reconciled us to one another. When she went home to be with Him, we had no issues with each other. My son does not have to live with the guilt of having had unresolved issues with his mother.

I know that there might be someone who says, "Bill you don't understand." "Bill you don't know what they did to me."

You might be absolutely right, but Jesus does. He knows it through experience and He knows it because He knows you. He is the High Priest who can be touched with our infirmities. He was tested in every way, yet He never sinned (in His heart or His flesh). Invite Him in. Let Him touch the wound. Let Him heal that broken heart. Let Him enable you to move on with your life.

There is always HOPE, when Jesus is in the picture.

# "For We Are Saved By Hope"

## Chapter 6

# Hope in Sickness

*"Be strong and of good courage, do not fear nor be afraid of them, for the Lord your God, He is the One who goes with you. He will not leave you nor forsake you."*
Deuteronomy 31:6

There are times in all of our lives we just *have* to trust the Lord. There will be times when we don't see Him, feel Him or hear Him. But He promised He would be there and that He would not forsake us. This does not mean that everything is going to work out the way that we want it to. To me, it means He will be there with us, every step of the way.

This chapter concerns something that I was connected to but not a victim of. It starts back in 1986 when my wife developed what appeared to be some type of arthritic condition. She went to several doctors and was finally diagnosed with what was first thought to be lupus. Later, it was determined that she had polio myositis, which is a type of arthritic condition that is closely associated with lupus. For the next eight years, she was treated with steroids. Though helpful, they had a devastating effect on her body.

Claudia was a small, petite woman. She was a great dancer and very independent. At the beginning of the condition, her dress size was about a woman's 6-8. During the time of taking the steroids, she grew to a size 16-18. It is something that would be devastating to most women. Not only that, she went through incredible mood swings. And to make matters even worse, she was in constant pain. While the medicine did provide some relief, this sickness never let up.

Her courage through those years was remarkable. She never stopped working. She never stopped going to church. She never stopped trusting God in the midst of all this craziness. She never gave up her faith in God, though she often wondered where He was in the midst of her turmoil. She seemed determined not to let this thing do her in.

I would pray for her. Ministers would pray for her. Nothing seemed to move this dreaded disease. Often, she and I both wondered where was "the Lord that heals thee." There came a point during this period when I wanted a divorce. I could not handle her mood swings any longer. One day, I stormed out of the house in a rage, vowing a divorce.

No sooner had I gotten to the bottom of the steps which led from the porch than the Lord spoke into my heart and said, "That is your flesh speaking. Get back in the house. She did not leave you when you were sick in sin."

I sheepishly walked back inside the house with my tail between my legs and asked her to forgive me for my attitude. The Lord also gave me another word during this time. He said as far as Claudia was concerned, "Where it's the medicine – understand it. Where it's Claudia, forgive her." Somehow, those words were able to take root in my heart and enabled me to hang in there.

At the end of eight years, Claudia decided to go to a new doctor. Just by visible observation, this doctor felt that Claudia's condition was not polymyositis after all. She believed that Claudia had Lyme's Disease, a disease that is spread by a deer tick. The area where we had lived was known to have had numerous cases of the disease. After testing, the doctors' assumptions turned out to be right.

However, Claudia had now been treated with steroids for a disease that should have been treated with antibiotics. The results were devastating. She was weaned away from the steroids and given the antibiotics. This caused a complication during Claudia's menstrual cycle. The blood would not clot and she had to have three blood transfusions to replace the blood she had lost. She had nearly bled to death.

Then, the doctors felt that she needed to have her spleen removed to get the blood to build up more white blood cells. In the midst of all of this, we wondered where God was and why was He allowing this to happen. However, by God's grace, she made it through.

I do not know of too many people who do not wonder where the Lord is when all hell seems to be breaking loose in their lives. The Bible is full of these folks. Often, you can get angry at the one who has all of the answers. By His grace, I don't think we got mad but we sure did wonder where He was. Or maybe we did get mad from time to time. But God can handle it!

A year or so after this ordeal, Claudia felt a lump in her breast. She went to the doctor and an X-ray revealed her worst fear. There was the possibility of cancer. The doctors wanted to perform a lumpectomy.

We allowed them to do that and awaited the results. It was a wait that seemed long though it only took a few days.

We were summoned to the doctor's office and our worst fears were confirmed. The doctors felt that the cancer was malignant. They also felt that the breast needed to be removed. It was at that point that the Lord again spoke into my heart and said, "Do not allow them to remove her breast."

As the doctor waited for our reply, she left Claudia and I in the office alone. I told Claudia what I felt the Lord had spoken into my heart. She concurred and was willing to do what we felt the Lord had said.

The doctor returned and we told her that we were not going to let them remove the breast. We also told them that they could do another lumpectomy and get as much of the cancer as possible and that we would rely on the Lord to get the rest.

Let me stop here by saying: I am not crazy. If I was not convinced that the Lord had spoken, we were willing to go through with the operation. The Bible says "According to your faith, be it unto you." I also feel that if it is not faith, it is foolishness. I was not willing to gamble with Claudia's life over something that might have amounted to nothing but foolishness.

The doctor looked at us as though we were crazy but she was willing to yield to our demands. A week or two later, Claudia went back in for the surgery. During that waiting period, I told as many people as possible to pray for us. I was working in a ministry with thousands of folks on staff.

Much to the surprise of the doctors, the cancer was completely gone! May the God of all creation be praised.

Claudia came home with a renewed faith and again, we saw the faithfulness of our God and the truth of His word.

By this time, we thought that the testing of our faith had come to an end. But not too long after that Claudia was not feeling well. It did not seem too serious. She continued to work. However, one Friday in March of 1997, she went to work and her friends and supervisor felt that she was looking too ill to stay at work. They told her that they believed it was best for her to go home. My oldest son, Randy, drove to her job, picked her up and brought her home. She immediately went upstairs and went to bed.

About an hour later, I was in the kitchen, paying some bills. In the 30 years of our marriage, I have never seen Claudia walk around the house in her underwear. She came down the steps in her underwear and went to the bathroom. As she went back to the bedroom, she reached on top of the refrigerator and took a hand filled with Cheerios out of the box and walked back upstairs. I asked her, "Claudia, what is the matter with you?" She answered in a childlike voice and said, "I'm eating Cheerios." I thought it was strange, but I continued back to the job of writing checks.

About 45 minutes later, she repeated the scene again. This time, I realized that there was something wrong. I told her she needed to go to the hospital. She quickly dismissed me as only she could. I called a friend of ours who was a nurse and told her to come to the house and tell Claudia to go to the hospital. She came over and simply said, "Claudia, I want you to go to the hospital."

Claudia immediately said, "OK." Those of you who are reading this know what that frustration is all about.

We arrived at the hospital at about 7 pm. Claudia was checked in and examined. The examination did not reveal anything in particular. She was told that she could go home and get some rest. I felt a little foolish but was still convinced that something was wrong. When Claudia went to sign the release papers, she was asked to place her signature at the bottom of the page. When she signed her name, she signed from the lower left hand corner to the top right hand corner. At that time, the attending nurse realized that something was indeed wrong.

A battery of blood tests were run. When the readings came back, they revealed that something had gone wrong with Claudia's liver. The normal reading should have been 1.4 or so. Claudia's reading was 19.3.

They immediately rushed her into the Intensive Care Unit. An attempt to contact our family doctor revealed that he was on vacation. His stand-in was contacted and she immediately came to the hospital. Upon her arrival, she checked with the doctors and nurses and quickly examined Claudia. A short time later, she came out and spoke to me. In her most professional and sensitive manner she said, "Mr. Paige, you had better prepare yourself for the worst."

In other words, she was telling me that she did not think Claudia was going to make it. It was an incredible shock that I was not expecting. That night, Claudia became delusional and had to be restrained in bed. What happened? Her liver had completely shut down. Because the liver is the filter of the human body, all kinds of toxins were being released into her bloodstream. The hospital personnel tied her down but she was somehow able to eat through the restraints.

On Sunday, she went into a coma. Her name was placed on a liver transplant list. However, the chances of her getting one were pretty slim in comparison to the number of people already on the list. The doctors had all kinds of tubes stuck in her body. Things were not looking good.

This is one of the lessons that I have learned in life: No matter how bad it is, it can always get worse. On Tuesday evening, my oldest son Randy and I were at the hospital. One of the doctors came to me and said, "If your wife does not get a liver by Thursday, she will be dead on Friday." He was very gracious in his explanation.

As a matter of fact, every doctor and nurse that we encountered in the Surgical Care Unit and the Intensive Care Unit at Mt. Sinai Hospital were the most wonderful folks in the profession of medicine that I have ever encountered. I will forever be thankful to them and all that they did to help Claudia as well as comfort my family and friends.

Randy and I left the hospital and stopped to get something to eat and talk over what was told to us. We did not know what to do. A short time later, we got in the car and began our drive back to our home in New Jersey. We were driving through Harlem in Manhattan. We were near 121$^{st}$ Street and 3$^{rd}$ Avenue when I felt what I thought might have been the Lord prompting me to call the hospital. I simply shrugged it off as wishful thinking on my part. When we reached 122$^{nd}$ Street, it seemed as though someone grabbed me in my solar plexus and said, "I said call the hospital."

I then knew for sure that it was the Lord. I told Randy, and I pulled over and went to a pay phone and called the nurse's station in the Intensive Care Unit.

When I identified myself, the nurse who answered the phone said, "Mr.Paige, thank God you got our message."

I got a message but it was not theirs. From the time we had left the hospital until we reached 122$^{nd}$ Street, a liver had been located for Claudia. In the midst of all the drama, the papers had not been signed for the transplant. We drove back to the hospital and signed the papers. Then, the only thing we could do was wait. This was late Tuesday evening.

All of this was taking place during the Lent Season. I had been scheduled to debate the Archdiocese Bishop of the Episcopal Church on Wednesday night. That was not as strange as the subject matter that we were going to discuss: DEATH. Ironically, he was unable to make the discussion and I had to speak alone. Here was Claudia literally standing at death's door, and I was preaching on death in the church. It almost seemed like a cruel joke. But I know that God is not a prankster. I believe that it was one of my better messages because it came from the depths of my heart.

You might ask, "How could he have been preaching when his wife was undergoing an operation which might have ended with her dying?"

My answer is simple. I could not have done anything in the operating room. All of that was in the hands of the Lord and the doctors and nurses He used that night. I had prayed and there were hundreds upon hundreds of other folks praying as well. I needed only to trust the Lord. I don't believe that I was some kind of mighty man of faith or anything close to that.

As a matter of fact, I believe that I was able to deal with all of this without falling apart simply because He sustained me.

I would have been a wreck if it had not been for Him. It has been one of the most dramatic times in my Christian experience. I was able to put my finger on His ability to take me through a trial such as this. It is something that cannot be explained adequately in words. I just know that He was there with my family and me every step of the way.

The operation was performed on Wednesday night. Claudia came out of the coma sometime on Thursday. When I came to see her on Friday, she said, "Paige, why did you let them take my liver?" She was completely unaware of how close she had come to dying nor did she have any recollection as to how sick she was prior to the operation.

Several days later, she told us that she went into the presence of the Lord during the ordeal. The Lord told her she could not come into heaven yet because she had not completed the job He had given her to do. In essence, she had been disobedient to the call to ministry.

I realize that all situations do not turn out the way we hope they will. Many times, things don't go the way we plan. However, one thing remains: GOD IS IN CONTROL! Nothing escapes His notice, nothing is impossible to Him (whether we believe it or not.) All power is in His hands. We are simply called to trust Him.

The Lord graciously gave Claudia 16 more years to go forth to do His bidding. Today, she is with Him in glory. Had it not been for His grace and mercy, she would have gone home quite a while before. All praise to the Living God who sits high and looks low. *His arms are not short that they cannot save or His ears dull that they cannot hear!!* (Psalm 138:6, Isaiah 59:1).

# "For We Are Saved By Hope"

## Chapter 7

# *Hope in Fear*

*"The lookout reported, He has reached them, but he isn't coming back either. The driving is like that of Jehu son of Nishi – he drives like a maniac."*
2 Kings 9:20 (NIV)

*"Jehu said, Come with me and see my zeal for the Lord. Then he had him ride along in his chariot."* 2 Kings 10:16 (NIV)

I don't know what you know about this story, but these verses speak for themselves. How would you like to have an invitation like that, knowing what the first verse has to say about Jehu? I share that to help you relate to what takes place in this chapter.

(Chuck Swindoll)

Have you ever felt paralyzed by fear or the hopelessness of a situation?

I call it being stuck. It is like being driven in a car by someone who does not drive that well. You know what I mean. You are sitting there with your eyes on the road. You are aware of the traffic all around you. You see the intersection as you approach.

You prepare to stop, but the person at the wheel seems to be in his or her own little world.

The light changes from green to yellow, and you know you are too far from the intersection to make it. The person is talking and looking all over the place while engaged in conversation, and you begin to step on brakes that don't exist. Finally, you scream at the top of your voice, and the car come to a screeching stop. You put your heart back in your chest where it belongs. There is no worse feeling than not being in control. It usually takes on the emotion of fear.

It was such a night in the middle of winter. I was working the midnight tour. I had been a police officer for about a year. My partner John had been on the job for about five years. He had been on the job long enough to have been assigned a Sector: a designated part of the jurisdiction that whoever was assigned was responsible for.

It was a rule that the senior man always drove the car. It was at his discretion if a partner would be allowed to drive. I had established a reputation for being a crazy driver. It would have been a sign of wisdom not to let me drive the car. That particular evening John was walking in the wisdom of God (though he didn't know it).

We were about an hour into the tour when I began a constant barrage of requests to drive. John had heard stories from other officers who had made the mistake of letting me drive. I had been in several hair-raising high-speed pursuits.

My attitude was, if I get involved in a pursuit, I was not stopping unless we ran out of gas or we had a real bad accident. I found nothing wrong with that philosophy. My partners did not agree.

Each time I asked John for the opportunity to drive the car, the answer was, "No." I would not be deterred. I would ask every 20 minutes or so. I figured I could wear him down. As I look back on that night, I was acting like a spoiled little brat that had to have his way.

Around four in the morning, I noticed that John was getting tired. I waited until I saw that he was having trouble staying awake.

I popped the question for about the 10th time. I was elated when he finally said, "OK you can drive." I tried not to show the enthusiasm of a 10-year-old kid who had been given a shopping spree at the local toy dealer. As I took the steering wheel in hand, I immediately began looking for speeders and traffic violators to stop. I was not so concerned with giving out tickets. I just liked pulling people over and using the siren.

John sat patiently in the passenger seat, often rolling his eyes. This went on for about an hour and a half. Finally, the night caught up with me and I pulled the car over on the shoulder of the road. The speed limit was 30 miles per hour. Much to John's relief, my little escapade had come to an end.

We were sitting there no more than five or six minutes when a car went by us at 80 or 90 miles per hour. He was so close to our car that it caused our car to rock as if someone were outside shaking it. As I reached for the gearshift, John now realized that he had made the biggest mistake of his life.

When I was on the police force, I had a nickname -- Satch. It was taken from Satchel Paige who played in the old Negro Baseball League. I used to pitch when I played baseball growing up as a kid.

I had a great fastball but little control. You took your life into your own hands when you had to face me.

John reached over and grabbed my wrist as I put the vehicle into drive. He said with fear in his voice, "Satch, forget it. You will never catch him."

I looked at him in anger and said, "Get your stinking hands off of me."

The chase was on. There was hardly any traffic on the road. I got the car up to about 70 when John started pleading with me to stop. He was screaming, "Stop it! Stop it! You are going to kill us!"

I screamed back at the top of my voice, "Shut up!" I promised him that if I had not caught this speeder within the next mile or so, I would break off the pursuit. I passed that mark in excess of 90 miles per hour.

By this time, it had become a personal issue, and I was not thinking about breaking the pursuit. John was now in full panic. As he slid down in the fire well of the passenger seat, he was pleading with me to stop. I again screamed for him to shut up. I almost lost control of the car a couple of times. But I could see that I was gaining on the speeder. About nine miles after we began, I pulled alongside of the vehicle with lights flashing and siren wailing. I motioned for him to pull over and he finally did. (This happened at a time when police could shoot at fleeing vehicles). I am so glad that he stopped.

As I approached the vehicle, I looked back to see if John was coming to back me up. What I saw still brings a smile to my face.

John was out of the police car and approaching the vehicle. He could barely walk. His eyes were bulging in their sockets. You could almost hear his knees knocking together. The look of fear was mixed with a look of anger. I could see that he wanted to hit me. But at that time, I was so filled with anger. And in the words of the TV character, Mr. T, "I would have beaten him like a drum." We ended up locking up the driver of the vehicle. We never knew why he was driving so fast.

Rest assured, from that day for the next 18 years, John never let me drive the car again. He literally left the marks from his fingernails in the dashboard. He would show them to guys to convince them of how scary the pursuit had been.

I know that is a long story to get to what I am trying to say. As I stated earlier, another way of looking at fear is being paralyzed. A simpler way of looking at being paralyzed is being stuck. I believe that there are places in our lives, if we are willing to examine them where we can acknowledge that we are stuck. We are unable to move on. We want to get control of a situation but we feel like John.

We are in the "passenger seat of life" with no possible way of bringing things under control. Worse yet (not like in the case of John during the pursuit), we go for the ride acting like we are not afraid or that we think we are in control.

We do this a lot to keep people from seeing the real us. I saw this often during my years in the police department. Mostly men, and some women, who acted like they were in control, but it did not take long for the real them to come to the surface. You are put in position to be in control of situations that you can't handle, when an overreaction to a situation will often be the result.

When Jesus was on the earth, He constantly dealt with people who were stuck.

There is the story in John 5 when Jesus finds some folk who were in bad shape hanging around a pool waiting for the "magic bullet." The word was out that an angel would come and trouble the water and the first person in the pool would be healed. The Bible says, *There is nothing new under the sun.* (Ecclesiastes 1:9) How often do we want an angel or God Himself to show up more or less and shoot us with the magic bullet?

On this day, Jesus comes along and sees a paralyzed man lying there. Jesus knows his condition and that his desire to be healed has obviously brought him. Or maybe he has requested for someone to bring him there. The Bible goes on to say that he has been coming there for 38 years. That's a long time to be stuck.

If you have been stuck, how long? In my crazy imagination, I wonder if the angel shows up, and he's paralyzed, how is he going to get in the pool in the first place? It's almost like a cruel joke. None of the other folks are going to help him because they are preoccupied with their own needs.

The great thing about Jesus is that He is always preoccupied with everyone else's needs. This day, Jesus looks at the man and asks, *Do you want to be made well?* (John 5:6)

What a crazy question to someone who doesn't know that the God of the universe is asking it. Maybe it is the first time in a long time that someone has shown any concern for him. Maybe he is just happy that someone would talk to him.

So he answers the question, *Sir, I have no man to put me into the pool when the water is stirred up; but while I am coming, another steps down before me.* (John 5:7)

The first time I read the story, I thought he never answered the question but had just made an excuse for himself. It hit me one day that he perfectly answered the question when he said, "When I am trying." That was enough for Jesus. He said to the man, "Pick up your bed and walk." And immediately, the man rose to his feet, holding his bed.

Wow, what a scene that must have been! What about all the people who knew this man? What about those who were gathered around the pool waiting for the angel? Did they know that the one speaking to the man had the power to dispatch the angel?

After catching some grief from some people who were more concerned with rules than miracles, the man goes to the temple to give thanks to God. Jesus reappears, identifies himself and gives a stern warning, *Go and sin no more lest something worse happens to you.* (John 5:14) Two great things take place here for me.

First of all, the man never knows who spoke into his life that day at the pool. It was not about faith in God in that instance. The man's face was grounded in getting in a pool that had been troubled by an angel. But he did have faith. God does respond to faith. But the same voice that spoke this world into existence was the voice that spoke into this man's pitiful condition. That voice had lost no power and to that voice, *This is an easy thing in the sight of the Lord.* (2 Kings 3:18)

Secondly, it seems that sin may have been a contributing issue for this man's paralysis. Seemingly, if there would be a return to that sin, something worse might happen. One thing that life has definitely taught me is this: no matter how bad it is, it can always get worse.

Where are you stuck? When Jesus tells you to go and sin no more, do you realize in an instant what He is talking about? We are stuck in so many ways, and we live in the fear of being found out. We are truly paralyzed and we need the God of the universe to meet us at our pool. There is nothing worse than living life out of control. Though we have no power in and of ourselves, the God of the universe, through the power of the Holy Spirit, is available to empower us to pick up our beds and walk. Walk and walk in freedom and the liberty that comes from turning from sin and not returning there. There is nothing worse than being powerless in a given situation.

One of the major things that Jesus did in His interactions with mankind was to empower them to deal with the crises of life. We simply need power over the things that have had power over us for so long. He said, *You shall have power after the Holy Spirit has come upon you.* (Acts 1:8) God has given us everything we need. We need only to avail ourselves to it. He does not want us to live our lives in fear. He does not want us paralyzed. Perfect love casts out fear. Fear is tormenting. (1 John 4:18) He wants us to live in total freedom. *For he who the Son sets free, they shall be free indeed.* (John 8:36) Are you free or are you paralyzed? Are you free or are you living in fear? Jesus Christ is the answer for both of these situations.

The night of the pursuit, John was fearful and he was paralyzed in that police car. Since that night, he has come to know Jesus as Savior and Lord. He has also come to know what perfect Love is and His ability to make a person Free!!!

## Chapter 8

# *Hope in Despair*

*"The thief does not come except to steal, and to kill, and to destroy. I have come that they may have life, and that they may have it more abundantly."* John 10:10

Have you ever wondered how many tragedies could be avoided if we would only obey the warnings? There is one truth about the word of God; it gives ample warnings on how to negotiate the treacherous waters of life. If we pay attention, we can avoid many of the pitfalls the enemy attempts to set up for our downfall.

One cold wintry evening, I was driving home on the New York State Thruway. From the outward appearance, things could not have been better. It looked like I was doing well in the ministry. The anointing of the Lord was flowing in my life. Many kids were turning their lives over to the Lord. I was well liked as a chaplain at Children's Village. People felt that I was a success as a husband and father. But deep on the inside, I knew better.

Sin had entrenched itself in my life. I found myself continually praying this prayer: "Father, I know I said, I wouldn't do it again, but I did. Please forgive me, AGAIN."

The prayer had become routine in my life. I had a great understanding of what Paul meant when he wrote, *The things I don't want to do, I do. Things that I want to do, I don't. When I desire to do good, evil is always present with me.* (Romans 7:20-21)

I knew those words well but had absolutely no understanding of what he was talking when he said, *"Now therefore there is no condemnation to those who are in Christ"* (Romans 8:1). However, the only thing I could focus on was the sin in my life. I was failing as a husband, father, son, and minister of the Gospel. I was a spiritual mess. It seemed like the only ones who truly knew what I was going through were me and the Lord. Thankfully, that was enough.

As a result of my ignorance, the evil one took full advantage. It is no wonder why the Bible says, *"For the lack of knowledge my people are destroyed."* (Hosea 4:6) At this point, Satan unleashed a diabolical plan to destroy my life. Most amazingly, the instrument of that destruction would be me.

As I traveled north on Interstate 87 in New York, I started driving across the Tappan Zee Bridge. It is a three-mile bridge located about 15 miles north of New York City and crosses the Hudson River between Westchester County and Rockland County.

On this night, the thoughts of hopelessness, helplessness, and worthlessness again filled my mind. I felt like I was the lowest of all of God's creation. There was no one as messed up as me as far as I was concerned.

I held a deep hatred and contempt for myself. This was not the first time that I had these thoughts running through my mind. It would be during these times that I would call myself all kinds of names (most preceded with or followed by profanity). I knew better but yet I was overwhelmed with these thoughts.

I had encouraged others when they shared with me the same plight in their lives. But the encouragements that I gave them rang hollow when I thought about myself.

I was about one third of the way across the bridge driving in the inside lane. I was driving a small car that night. I was coming up on an eighteen-wheeler. A thought came into my mind. "Why don't you drive under the wheels of the truck?"

For whatever reason, that thought made perfect sense. Just as I was about to do it, another thought came into my mind. This thought was not overpowering, but it seemed so real. The thought came as if it were spoken by someone trying to tell me something. It simply said, "This is how the devil deceives my children into committing suicide." And that was all. However, those words spoke volumes into my life. The word seemed to say so much more than what the words reflected.

First of all, I am completely convinced that the thoughts were the thoughts of my Heavenly Father. I and I alone will stand before Him and He will judge me. His words said that He was far more concerned about me than the issues of my life. It did not mean that the issues of my life were not important (because they were), but that I was more important to Him.

They also said that I needed to get off of that bridge and really begin to deal with those issues.

As I exited the bridge, I was excited to begin my life afresh. Again, I asked the Lord for forgiveness, and this time I received it. It was a new chapter in my life.

I would also like to mention that at the time of this incident, I was ministering at a church in Manhattan. I had replaced a minister who had committed suicide. I know nothing of the events surrounding that suicide, but I often wonder if the same forces that had pitted themselves against that minister had come to take advantage of me in my weakness. I don't know but I wonder. Even during my days in the police department, suicides would seem to come in clusters.

I often think of that night and compare it to the night that Jesus was betrayed. He warned Peter that night that Satan had asked to have him that he might sift him (Peter) as wheat. Peter was also told that he should strengthen the brethren after his conversion. Like most of us, Peter didn't get the message. He began to boast of his courage and steadfastness in defending Christ even to the point of death. It was only a short time later that evening when he denied Jesus with cursing and the accompaniment of a rooster. The Bible tells us that Peter ran and wept bitterly. (Luke 22:31-62) When we think that we stand we are warned to take heed lest we fall. (1 Corinthians 10:12)

I wonder how long I ignored the signs. I was continually ignoring the promptings of the Holy Spirit, continually allowing my heart to be hardened by the deceitfulness of sin. I wonder how many times I allowed my success in ministry to cloud my own eyes from the hypocrisy in my own life. I believe that any one of these and so many more are the things that can lead to one's ruination in Christ.

I once wrote a poem that contained these words:

"YOU WILL STAND IN THE RUIN OF YOUR
OWN DOIN,'
SCRATCHING YOUR HEAD IN WONDER."

I thank God so much for His willingness to put up with us, willing that we would come to repentance and not perish, as His word states in 2 Peter 3:9.

I also wonder if I would have really driven my car under the wheels of the truck that night. I can't say for sure. However, I am absolutely convinced that the Lord thought it was important enough for Him to speak into my heart that night. I reason that if it was important enough for Him to have to speak to me there was a good chance that I might have carried out the evil desires of the evil one. Regardless, I am happy that I am here to write this book.

A couple of weeks later, I was driving on the Tappan Zee Bridge again. This time, I was going in the opposite direction. Christ said to Peter, *When you are converted, strengthen the brethren.* (Luke 22:32) The word "converted" in this context simply means to go in the opposite direction. It was a couple of days before I was to leave for a trip to the Ukraine. I was late for work and was speeding.

Again, I was coming up on an eighteen-wheeler that was driving the speed limit. I thought I saw something flying through the air. At that moment, I heard a voice that was so powerful yet, not yelling. I could not tell you if my life depended on it, if the voice was in my mind or audible. It said, "Turn your head." I turned my head to the right, looking south down the Hudson River. I could see the George Washington Bridge about 18 miles away.

I was almost exactly opposite the place where just a couple of weeks earlier I heard that wonderful voice of encouragement. In light of what happened next, it is amazing what the word converted means as explained above.

At this point, a metal bar comes crashing through the windshield of my car. It embeds itself in the dashboard and lodges itself behind the speedometer. I had glass in my hair and in my ear. All this took place in a matter of seconds.

However, I did not get a scratch, and my eyes were saved from getting glass in them as well. A woman was driving a car immediately to my left. She saw the whole thing and had a look of horror on her face. I said to myself, "Why is she making a face? She is not in the accident."

Later, I found out what had happened: that metal bar was attached to the mud flap located at the left rear wheel of the truck and it had broken off. When it hit the road, it separated from the flap, bounced into the air and came through my windshield. I wonder what would have happened if I were driving a little faster or a little slower. Possibly, there might have been no book to read.

I caught up with the truck driver at the tollbooth and pulled up next to him with this javelin sticking out of my windshield. I rolled my window down on the passenger side and yelled to him, "Hey! This belongs to you."

There was a look of surprise and shock on his face. We paid our tolls and pulled over to the side of the road. He got out of his truck and walked back to my car. I could see that by now he was shaken as he realized the extent of the danger. His knees were literally shaking. However, I was incredibly calm.

I was not shaken at all. As a matter of fact, the peace of God had invaded every part of my mind. At this point, the driver of the truck got angry about the fact that I am not upset.

This was how I felt about the whole incident. If I am wrong then I and only I will have to answer to the Lord. It was like what I call a "Holy Ghost Kodak Moment." I sensed that it was God letting me know that if He ever wanted to get rid of me, there would be no problem. However, there were some issues in my life that had to go.

I believe that about all of us. There are things that the Lord is trying to get out of our lives, and He will exhaust Himself to do it. The easy road or the hard road is our choice. It seems like every road that I take is the hard road. I am so glad that He is there as well.

In ending this chapter, the truck driver turned out to be a young man who had walked away from the Lord. We prayed together and He asked the Lord to take His rightful place in his heart. I never heard from him again. But it goes to show that the Lord works all things together for the good to those who are called according to His purpose (Romans 8:28). In Psalm 51, David writes, *"and sinners will be converted unto thee."*

First, He got me and then He got the truck driver. All as a result of my despair. I would rather be telling stories of how the Lord did great things in the midst of my total surrender to Him. That is not the case in this story. However, He still did great things!! He never gives up on us. He relentlessly pursues us. It is His goodness that leads us to repentance. His goodness, not His wrath; though both can accomplish the same thing.

Thank God when He uses His goodness.

# "For We Are Saved By Hope"

## Chapter 9

# *Hope on the Mission Field*

*"And He said to them, Go into all the world and preach the gospel to every creature."* Mark 15:16
*"But you shall receive power when the Holy Spirit has come upon you; and you shall be witnesses to Me in Jerusalem, and in all Judea and Samaria, and to the end of the earth."* Acts 1:8

Spring, 1992:

I had just come out of a dark period in my walk with the Lord. Yet, the Bible says that it is the goodness of the Lord that leads to repentance. (Romans 2:4) In spite of my fall, God was fulfilling his call on my life. More importantly, He was proving His faithfulness to me through His word.

I had gone to the Ukraine shortly after my "fall off the wall." I was with a team from a church on Long Island.

We were visiting some rural communities and sharing the gospel of Christ. God was doing amazing things.

On this day, we were speaking in a town called Bulgakovo. It was an outdoor service near the village square. To this day, I do not remember how or why things were done in the fashion that they were. We sang songs. The people who had a relationship with Jesus were on one side of the street and those who didn't were on the other side.

I preached the gospel that day and people crossed from the other side of the street to our side. They were warmly accepted into the family of God. I had not given much thought to that arrangement until recently. I wonder how those who had decided not to receive Christ felt. Was it a guilt trip of some type? Did the people of the town continue to love them and pray for them? Did the church pray for those people? Did more come to the Lord as a result of the change they saw in the lives of those who had entered into a relationship with Christ? I don't know, but I wonder about that now.

When I finished speaking, I noticed some of the elders of the local church talking to a woman. She was an older, stout Ukrainian woman dressed in traditional Ukrainian clothes.

Every once in a while, the elders would turn and look at me. Then, they would continue talking to the woman. I could see that she was crying. I could tell that the conversation had something to do with me. I thought I must have said something that offended this woman. It is just like me to think the worst case scenario.

Finally, they brought the woman over to me so I could meet her.

We were introduced through an interpreter. She told me an incredible story about her life. In 1945, this woman was in a Nazi concentration camp, slated to be executed. As the war was drawing to an end, the camp was liberated by black American soldiers. God had spared her life along with the remaining prisoners in the camp. I don't know where this took place or any of the other circumstances.

This woman had prayed for 45 years that God would send a black American to her town so that she could say thank you. After 45 years, I was the first black American she had ever seen. Remember, this was rural Ukraine. She thanked me for the kindness with which those men entreated her. We melted in each other's arms, crying together. Through what she was feeling, the Lord was also healing me from some of the racial scars that I had received in my life.

Some of those scars happened as early as the first grade, when I sent a Valentine's Day card to a girl in my class who was white. When her parents found out, she was not allowed to send cards anymore. It happened in the south, when my parents took me to Tennessee and West Virginia. I would have to drink from a separate water fountain; I was denied access to a hotel and made to go in the rear entrance of a theater.

At that time, I really did not understand what was going on, but I do now.

- It happens when playing Little League baseball and you are not allowed to play on a team, though you have better abilities than others on that team.

77

- It happens in the military when you find out that the Civil War still rages in the minds of some.

- It happens in the police department when you see overt racism towards some citizens and covert racism toward yourself.

- It happens on the streets when you watch fear on someone's face just because your color is not like theirs.

- Lastly, I have seen it in the church when the color of our skin keeps us separated from one another.

And let me be the first to say, it happens when you have it yourself, and you justify it because you have been hurt so many times. The bottom line is all hatred is wrong. There is no get out of jail free card for it, especially for those who call on the name of Christ. But the wounds are there. And they have to be healed. Why? Because hurting people hurt people.

But most importantly, God again showed his goodness to me that in spite of myself, He loved me. It is that kind of goodness that I have experienced in so many different ways. He still demonstrates that love to me over and over. In the good times, as well as in the bad.

On that day in the Ukrainian village, we sat down and had a great feast symbolic of the one we will have in heaven. It will not matter what your name is. It will not matter where you came from and it will not matter what your skin color is.

We will all be one great big loving family.

I have since heard that the woman has gone on to be with the Lord. A day will come when I will see her again. We have a lot in common. We have both been liberated from the concentration camp of sin and hate. We have been liberated by the greatest liberator of all time. His name is Jesus. He is still setting captives free. Those who have been marked for death have been given a second chance. And in that chance, we have received eternal life. We will see that Jesus. And not only that; we will spend eternity with Him.

So Father, this day I thank you for your steadfast love that never ceases and your mercy that never comes to an end. It is new every morning. Great is your faithfulness, Oh, Lord, great is your faithfulness.

I don't even know that woman's name. Today, it is not important. She is with you now, Lord. There will come a day when we will be reunited. Then, we will hug again and I will never forget her name.

# "For We Are Saved By Hope"

## Chapter 10

# *Hope in a Storm*

*"Then they cry out to the Lord in their trouble. And He brings them out of their distresses. He calms the storm, So that its waves are still. Then they are glad because they are quiet; So He guides them to their desired haven. Oh, that men would give thanks to the Lord for His goodness And for His wonderful works to the children of men."*
Psalm 107:28-31

Life is filled with ups and downs. Often, we don't know how we're going to make it. Then we find ourselves on the other side of what we presumed were overwhelming circumstances. We can only attribute the answer to the Lord. He just says one thing: Read verse 31 very carefully. He has an expectation of gratitude.

I love the fact that Jesus said, "In this world you are going to have trouble." (John 16:33) He tells us in advance. I believe it is a warning so that when trouble comes, we are not dismayed. He also tells us so that we have peace in Him. Most importantly, He reminds us that He has overcome the world. What words of both warning and comfort! A reminder of who it is we are called to follow! (John 16:33)

There is an incredible story found in the fourth chapter of the book of Mark beginning at verse 35. It is a day that Jesus tells His disciples, *Let's cross over to the other side of the lake.* In other words, Jesus wanted to take them someplace. Since the day that I gave my life to the Lord, it seems like He is always trying to take me somewhere. Unfortunately, I have not always been willing to go. I love what the Bible says in verse 35 in the Philips' Translation; *"On the evening of THAT day..."*(emphasis added). It says *"That* day."

We all probably have some significant "that days" in our lives. Those are days that stand out more than others. I remember where I was when John F. Kennedy was assassinated. I remember where I was on 9/11. I remember where I was when my sons were born. I remember where I was when I proposed to my wife. I remember the day I scored two touchdowns in my last high school football game. There are so many days that stand out more or seem to be more significant than others. I believe this is one of those days for the disciples. It is a day that would forever build their faith in Jesus. It is a day that they would probably look back on and still scratch their heads.

The day starts out as an ordinary day for them. Jesus has been teaching from a boat. As usual, people are riveted by His words. Upon finishing His teaching, He turns to His crew (the disciples) and simply says, *Let's cross over to the other side* (of the lake). Mark 4:35

The sun is beginning to set. Maybe the temperature's a high 85, and there's not a cloud in the sky. The lake is like crystal. The sun glistens off the face of the lake. A moderate breeze begins to kick up.

Jesus is tired from all the ministry He has been involved in that day. He goes to sleep on a mat and leaves the travel arrangements to the disciples. After all, they are fisherman. They have crossed the lake many times.

The wind begins to pick up and fills the sail. What starts as a moderate breeze has now turned into a full-fledged storm. Water begins to come into the boat. The disciples, with Peter as their leader, begin to bail water for their lives. The last place they want to end up is in the lake, swimming for their lives.

The remarkable thing in this story is that Jesus is still asleep. He is oblivious to all that is taking place around him. Maybe He is having sweet dreams while His friends are experiencing a nightmare of a storm.

There is another man in the Bible who sleeps through a storm. I believe his sleep is not a sleep of peace but one of frustration and anguish because of his disobedience to the Lord. His name is Jonah. The story can be found the first chapter of the book of Jonah. He was on the run from God. It is a deep sleep. Not one of contentment, but one of guilt and shame.

That is not the case with Jesus. His sleep is undisturbed. He is simply tired from all the ministry He has been doing in the Father's will. He is living a life of perfect obedience as recorded in Philippians 2. God the Father would describe Him as, *My beloved Son, in whom I am well pleased.* (Matthew 3:17)

Until now, the disciples are preoccupied with keeping the boat afloat. I believe they are bailing frantically when Peter notices that Jesus is asleep. He turns to Him and yells, *Master, don't you care that we are perishing?* (Mark 4:38) I wonder if Jesus was included in the "we?" Did they not realize that Jesus is also in the boat with them? Did they not realize that their lot would be His as well? Had they forgotten that He had said, "We are going over to the other side?" I don't know. However, I notice when things don't go well, we accuse others of not caring or not being concerned -- that even includes God.

Jesus rises from his interrupted sleep. Maybe with a small yawn. While looking at His disciples, He says, *Peace be still.* (Mark 4:39) With those simple words, He rebukes the wind and calms the sea.

He accomplished three things:

- He shuts the storm down
- He deals with the effects of the storm
- He turns His attention to His disciples

He simply asks them, "Where is your faith? Why did you doubt?" He never gets an answer to that question.

But another question is posed by the disciples, *Who is this, that even the waves obey Him?* (Mark 4:41) It is a question that is not easily answered to everyone's satisfaction. But one thing is for sure: He is more than just a teacher. He is more than just someone who sleeps through the storms that others are facing. He is definitely someone who cares. And not only does He care, He is able to do something.

He is God in the flesh. It is a mystery, as stated in the Bible, but the evidence is clear. The same voice that spoke the universe into existence, speaks to that storm and tells it to shut up. And it does.

Beyond a shadow of a doubt, every believer is going to have an assortment of "*that* days" in their lives. They will serve as reminders of what He has done in the past and what He is able to do in the future.

Maybe we read this story and say, "Jesus is good with the weather. What about the storms that rage in my life? Where is God when things are totally out of control? Does He have the ability to stop the storms in my life? I *hope* that the God of the universe is there for me when I have to face the storms of life."

This is something we will take a look at in the next two chapters. The Bible says, *So then faith comes by hearing and hearing by the word of God.* (Romans 10:17) *Without faith, it is impossible to please the Lord.* (Hebrews 11:6)

*Remember*: He has but to speak a word. We don't really know Who it is we have gotten ourselves connected to. More importantly, we don't know Who has connected Himself to us. He said, *You did not choose me, I chose you!* (John 15:16)

# "For We Are Saved By Hope"

## Chapter 11

# Hope through a Storm

*"Oh Lord God of hosts, Who is mighty like You, O Lord? Your faithfulness also surrounds You. You rule the raging of the sea; when its waves rise, You still them."* Psalm 89:8-9

We read in the preceding chapter about "that day" that Jesus quieted the storm as well as the heart of His disciples. We love the movies when at the last minute the hero seemingly comes from nowhere, riding his white horse, and carries out the rescue.

Men like movies when the good guys are pinned down and then off in the distance, they hear the sound of the bugle and the cavalry arriving to vanquish the enemy. We love it when the underdog is losing a game and then brings about an incredible upset. Those things are nice in sports, war and the movies. However, that is not how it always goes in life.

The disciples are doing all they can to keep their boat afloat in Mark 4. Jesus arises, lifts His voice and gives two commands and all is saved. The storm is stilled and the lake returns to crystal. Remember, the Bible says there was a great calm (Mark 4:39).

In real life, things don't always work out that way. Yet, God is in charge. We often put an expectation on Him that does not always work out the way we want. Personally, I like the way the story goes in Mark 4. However, my experience in Christ has looked a little different. Regardless, the Lord was in control.

I am thrilled that God has put the following story in the Bible. Though I have seen miracles like what happens in Mark 4, what happens in Matthew 14 has been more like my experience.

Jesus has just finished feeding the 5,000. It is time for them to be dismissed. Before He sends the crowd home, He orders the disciples to get into their boat and cross over to the other side of the lake. Then He dismisses the crowd who are now full of bread and fish as well as the word of God. At that time, as was His custom, He goes to a solitary place to spend time with His Father.

Jesus continually spends time with the Father. If it is important for Him, how much more important for us to do the same? I believe that it is a demonstration of why He is always ready to handle anything that would come His way.

As He comes out of prayer, He is quite alone. He looks to the sea and is able to make out His disciples in the distance. They have found themselves in a storm again. The Bible tells us that the wind was contrary to them. In other words, they were trying to go in one direction but the wind was opposing them, preventing their progress. They were stuck.

I wonder if Peter or one of the other disciples who was with Jesus on "that day" stood up and said, "Peace be still."

If that happened, it seemingly had no effect on the story. Have you ever tried to muster up all the energy you had to change a situation and nothing happened? How did that feel? Or maybe you had prayed for someone else and saw God move on their behalf, but when you needed a prayer answered, nothing happens. It feels like Heaven is closed and the Lord is on a vacation. If that is the case for you, welcome to my world.

Jesus seemingly is not moved by the situation. He does not go into panic mode as His friends strain at the oars and sails, but He delays before He begins His historic walk across the lake.

It is dark now. The storm is raging and the disciples are stuck in a storm that will not let them pass. However, the storm has no effect or power over Jesus. I wish I could have seen exactly what that looked like that night. In the midst of the mayhem, one of the disciples peers out and sees a figure walking on the water. Of course, many of these men are acquainted with the sea and storms. But they are not acquainted with someone walking on the water. Immediately, they go to the worst scenario. They cry out in fear, "It's a ghost!" (Matthew 14:26)

I love this part of the story. Jesus responds with these words: *Be of good cheer! It is I; do not be afraid.* (Matthew 14:27)

His voice is a voice of comfort. It is not the voice of a ghost. They did not recognize the figure on the lake, but they recognized His voice. Jesus says, *My sheep know my voice* (John 10:27). There is a very important lesson to be learned here. It is so necessary to recognize the voice of the Savior.

For there are many voices out there that would love to lead us astray.

For sure, Peter hears that voice and recognizes it. He responds, *Lord, if it is you, command me to come out on the water.*(Matthew 14:28) I don't fully understand the first part of Peter's response, but I somewhat get the second part. If Jesus "commands" us to do something, He has to be the one who enables us to do it. For His word says in John 15:5 *"Without Me, you can nothing."*

But, of course, the Bible goes on to say, *I can do all things through Christ who gives me the strength.* (Philippians 4:13)

Even though that verse had not been incorporated into the scriptures as of that time, the principle was in operation. For God is the same yesterday, today and forevermore. (Hebrews 13:8). And Peter comes down out of the boat and he begins walking towards Jesus. (Matthew 14:25)

Have you ever wondered what that must have been like? As far as we know, there is only one other man in the world who had done that: He was standing on the lake waiting for Peter. I think Jesus has a smile on His face. There is nothing in the scripture to support that, but I think that He is well pleased that His friend has the courage to trust Him to do what no other man had ever done. I also think it puts a smile on Jesus' face when we trust Him. It's when things don't seem to make any sense and we just simply trust Him.

Have you ever wondered what the other disciples were thinking? Were they simply awestruck or struck with fear and paralyzed?

I think that every once in a while, Peter got on the other disciples' nerves. I wonder if one or two of them wanted him to go down. As a direct note, this has nothing to do with Peter and what is happening on the lake. But I think there are people who want to see the followers of Jesus go down for the count because we simply do through faith what they would never do. Just a thought.

The storm is raging. The wind is howling and still pushing against the boat. In the midst of it all, two figures are outlined on the lake. Peter is making his way towards Jesus. That is how it usually starts off.

We are excited to put our faith in Him and He is smiling. As we trust Him, just for a moment, we take our eyes off of Him. We begin to look at the circumstances surrounding our situation. We start off in faith, but that faith quickly turns to sight. First of all, we notice that the storm is still raging. Jesus is not moving in the way that we have anticipated, affirming that Jesus cannot be put in the box. He has not told the storm to cease and the waves to calm themselves. He simply said, "Come." He has made no promise as to how things would work out. He has made no promise that He would stop the raging storms. He has spoken aloud and said, "Come."

But what He hasn't said aloud is, "Just trust me. Just believe."

We are not crazy about this course of action. We want the instant miracle that He performed during another storm. But Jesus is not in a box.

Peter begins to listen to the howling wind. The water from the waves begins to dampen his clothes. He has to squint because of the water in the air. He takes his eyes off of Jesus. The moment he does that, he begins to sink. Notice, he does not go under the water immediately. He has now turned into a human submarine. He cries out to Jesus in fear and panic. He says the first thing that comes to his mind: "Lord, save me." (Matthew 14:31)

Though the scripture in Romans 10:13 has not been written, he yells to Jesus to save him. By the way, that scripture says, *"Whosoever will call upon the name of the Lord shall be saved."* And it happens. Jesus saves him. An arm with muscles and a hand with callouses (of a carpenter by trade) reaches out to the sinking fisherman. He grabs Peter's hand and lifts him back upon the waves. He then walks him back to the boat. But before they begin their walk, Jesus says to His friend, *O you of little faith. Why did you doubt?* (Matthew 14:31).

I also believe that when Jesus asks this question, He is looking Peter in his eyes. Again, I believe (though I cannot prove it), Jesus has a smile on His face. It is not a smile that mocks. I believe it is a smile that approves of someone who at least has begun to trust Him. Jesus knows that there will come a time when Peter's faith will be more perfected than on the night of the storm. But this is one of the building blocks to a great beginning in faith.

Soon, they are back in the boat and the wind has ceased. In other words, Jesus does not stop this storm until the lesson has been learned. I have found that often God will not stop the storm because He knows the importance of learning to go through a storm.

We often want deliverance while the Lord wants development. Deliverance comes with a neat little bow attached to it. Development, on the other hand, is often dirty. We don't know what to do. It's like being on a roller coaster ride with no control. Once that ride starts, there is no turning back. It will be over when it is over. That is often what development looks like. When you come out on the other side, you only know one thing as an absolute truth: Jesus was there all the time.

The moment the wind ceases on that roller coaster of a night, the disciples all come and worship Jesus. There is no other reference where all the disciples come and worship Jesus all at the same time. Wow!!

He is worthy of that worship, whether it be theirs or ours. He has the ability to bring us out of any circumstance. He simply says, "Come." And when we come, as we must, He smiles and though we might not hear it, He says, "Trust me."

They all arrive on the other side of the lake. When they do, the people of that community recognize Jesus and bring out all the people who are sick. And many of those people who touch His garment are healed. Maybe I am pressing this point, but I wonder how many times others might have glanced at Peter in appreciation of the fact that He trusted Jesus.

That is all Jesus wants us to do. Trust Him, both in the storm and through the storm! Jesus is not the eye of the storm; He is the eye *in* the storm.

# "For We Are Saved By Hope"

## Chapter 12

# *Hope with Our Storms*

*"And we know that all things work together for good to those who love God, to those who are the called according to His purpose."* Romans 8:28

*"Thank God, the Father of our Lord Jesus Christ, that he is our Father and source of all mercy and comfort. For He gives us comfort in our trials so that we in turn may be able to give the same sort of strong sympathy to others in theirs. Indeed, experience shows that the more we share Christ's suffering the more we are able to give of his encouragement. This means that if we experience trouble we can pass on to you comfort and spiritual help; for if we ourselves have been comforted we know how to encourage you to endure patiently the same sort of troubles that we have ourselves endured. We are quite confident that if you have to suffer troubles as we have done, then, like us, you will find the comfort and encouragement of God."*
2 Corinthians 1:3-7 (Phillips Translation)

One amazing thing I find with God is that He leaves no stone unturned. He works with everything that happens in our lives.

Regardless of how tragic the events in our lives are (whether something we've done or have done to us) He has the ability to work it for good. In regards to what you are about to read, who would have believed that the Lord would call me to speak all over the world to what I believe is the most broken generation of young people known to mankind? He is utterly amazing.

So far in this book, we have taken a look at what Jesus does in a storm. He stops them or He enables us to get through them. In reading the accounts of those stories, we might say that Jesus is pretty good with the weather, but what about the storms that rage on the inside of my heart? What about the memories of things I have done and the things that have been done to me? What about the deep dark secrets that I harbor that cause me to visit the pit from time to time? What about the behavior that I cannot stand that comes rolling out of me from time to time? How does He handle those storms? Some of those storms are raging and some are quiet. But they are storms nonetheless.

One Bible story that has captured my heart is found in Luke 5:1-11. It is the story of Jesus calling some of the disciples to follow Him. He has commandeered Peter and his fishing boat to have a "Bible class" on the shore of the Sea of Gennesaret. No one knows what He speaks about that day. The sermon is not for us. It is for the people on the beach and those fishermen He will call who would later turn the world upside down. Peter is one of those fishermen. He is my favorite disciple. I would call him the "knucklehead" of the disciples. What I appreciate about him the most is that he is "real." He is not always right, but he is always "real."

On this day, Peter sees Jesus do something utterly amazing. At a time of day when the fishing should be over, Jesus allows the fishermen to catch more fish at one time than they probably have ever done in all their lives.

It happens in verses 7 and 8. They catch so many fish that their boats begin to sink. In verse 8, Peter comes to the reality that he is in the presence of someone so much greater than himself. Earlier, Peter addresses Jesus as Master (Teacher). But now he addresses Him in a completely different way.

He throws himself at the feet of Jesus and says, *Depart from me, for I am a sinful man, O Lord.* (Luke 5:8)

For Peter, the man Jesus has become more than just a teacher; He has become Lord. And Lord He is. I think if I could translate what Peter is really trying to say, it would sound something like this: "Lord, if you knew what kind of man I *really* am, you would have nothing to do with me."

What Peter doesn't realize is that Jesus knows exactly who he *really* is. It amazes me that Jesus did not say, "Then repent, you sinner. For the Kingdom of God is at hand (literally). No, Jesus simply says, *Do not be afraid. From now on, you will catch men.* (Luke 5:10)

I believe another unspoken message would have been, "Don't worry about the sinful stuff. If you get real close to me, you will change." So, Peter and his friend come to shore and forsake all to follow Jesus. In other words, they come as they are. They do not know that Jesus is beginning a good work in them, or that He would not stop until Peter was complete.

This is exactly how it is with those of us who choose to follow Jesus. We come just as we are. We come with excess baggage. I love this expression by Max Lucado (though I am not quite sure where I first heard it): "GOD LOVES YOU EXACTLY AS YOU ARE, BUT HE REFUSES TO LEAVE YOU THAT WAY."

When I gave my life to Jesus on December 26, 1980, I came just as I was. I had quite a bit of baggage and a lifestyle to prove it. The problem was that I had no idea of how much baggage I was carrying. The total deliverance from alcohol and substance abuse deceived me into thinking that I had arrived. I thought, what else was needed?

Little did I know that it was just the beginning. As I look back over the years, I can see that the Lord does not rush through the process of ridding us of that baggage. I now believe that the instant delivery from alcohol and substance abuse had nothing to do with sin. Though I believe very strongly that the wrongful use and abuse of those substances is sin, I think the Lord was taking away my pain killers. He was showing me that life is painful and you cannot keep running from it by sedating yourself. Other issues in my life fell by the wayside as well as I continued to steadfastly follow Him (easier said than done).

The story I shared earlier in this book when I wanted to bite off the nose of the man who insulted me when I was a police officer, was evidence of my brokenness. However, I did not realize it that night. I was at the early beginning of my journey.

************

When I began working at Children's Village, I was a member of a Pentecostal church.

Looking back on my experience in that church, I believe that there was more focus on spiritual gifts and not too much focus on spiritual issues. This meant you could have all kinds of spiritual issues in your life that would be covered over with charisma.

I did not realize it at the time, but some issues were beginning to surface from time to time. Unfortunately, I shrugged them off because the Lord was doing great things with the CV kids. I really regret that to this date. I thought the Lord had brought me to CV to be the deliverer. I did not know how much I needed to be delivered. Much development would need to take place before much deliverance would take place.

It seemed like I was quitting the job every week or so. It was amazing that the Lord kept me there for 14 years. At first, I did not realize how much I was like the kids there. Looking back, the Lord gave me 300 little Bill's to work with so that I might see myself in them.

## "For We Are Saved By Hope"

## Chapter 13

# *Hope in His Struggle*

*"So they arrived on the other side of the lake in the country of the Gadarenes. As Jesus was getting out of the boat, a man in the grip of an evil spirit rushed to meet him from the tombs where he was living. It was no longer possible for any human being to restrain him even with a chain. Indeed, he had frequently been secured with fetters and lengths of chain, but he had simply snapped the chains and broken the fetters in pieces. No one could do anything with him. All through the night as well as in the day-time he screamed among the tombs and on the hill-side, and cut himself with stones. Now, as soon as he saw Jesus in the distance, he ran and knelt before him, yelling at the top of his voice."* Mark 5:1-6

I am very thankful for the stories that God includes in the Bible. Sometimes, I've tried to imagine myself there as those events unfolded. Those stories have not only helped to produce faith in my life, but they have also given me great encouragement as well. Often, I have asked (myself and God), "Why did you put this or that in the Bible?"

The only answer I can come up with is because He knows that I will need it. The stories of David, Moses, Joshua, Rahab, Gideon, Paul, Peter, Mary and so many others have given me both hope and great resolve to continue in the faith.

I am also given hope when I read the stories of others who are not mentioned by name. While their names are not mentioned by God, they do have names. They are personal to Jesus. He touches their lives in the most profound ways. One of those stories is about a man who is living in a storm. In fact, I think it would be classified as a tornado.

Jesus and His disciples have just come out of a storm on the lake. He has powerfully demonstrated His power by calling out to a storm, ordering the winds to cease and the waves to be still. His disciples are in awe. They arrive safely on the other side of the lake. The wonder of who this can be is heavily on their minds.

As the boat is pulled safely to shore, they receive an unfriendly greeting that is and filled with rage. The Bible describes it this way in the scripture from Mark recorded above.

Other Gospels say that there were two men or that he was naked or that the road was not safe to travel because of their behavior. Obviously, both of them have issues.

But I don't want to focus on both of these men – just the one mentioned above. Satan had gotten his hooks into the life of this one. As a result, he is the victim of the one who comes to steal, kill and destroy.

Can you imagine the scene? Can you imagine the looks on the disciples' faces? I wonder if one of them might have suggested to Jesus that they should get back into the boat and cross back over the lake. Probably not. I have suggested it, however, as if I were there.

Then, to make matters worse (from a purely human standpoint), the demon in this man speaks out to Jesus and says, "What have you got to do with me, Jesus, Son of the most high God? For God's sake, don't torture me!"

Wow! This demon knows who Jesus is. The story reveals that he is afraid of Jesus and of what Jesus might do to him. He knows who Jesus is (and yet His disciples don't seem to know who He is in the storm) Mark 4:41. The Bible says that Jesus has already told the demon to come out. Then, Jesus asks the demon what his name is. He answers, *My name is Legion, for we are many.* (Mark 5:9) It seems that the demon is more concerned about what Jesus is going to do with him than he is about being cast out.

He implores Jesus to allow all of these demons to enter into a herd of pigs, which are nearby. Jesus allows this and those pigs run violently down a hill and drown in the sea. The Bible says the men who are in charge of the pigs flee to the city and the country and tell everyone what has happened.

Maybe it is my inquisitive nature, I don't know. But what are the disciples doing when all of this is happening? Were they staring with their mouths wide open? Or maybe they just keep glancing at each other in disbelief and wonderment. I don't know, but something incredible has taken place on that beach that day.

There is a lot more that happens that the Bible does not mention. When all of the townspeople arrive, the man who has been no less than a terror to anyone near that cemetery is sitting at the feet of Jesus. He wore clothes and he was in the right mind. I love the things that the Lord leaves for our holy imagination to perhaps fill in the blanks. These are my thoughts:

1. How long did it take for all the people to get to the cemetery?
2. What did Jesus do after he delivered the man from the demonic possession?
3. How did the man get into the predicament that allowed the demons to possess him?
4. What had gone wrong in his life?
5. Who may have abused him?
6. Who may have betrayed him?
7. Who may have violated him?
8. Who may have rejected or abandoned him?
9. Who may have neglected him?
10. Who may have falsely accused him of something?

It may be any of the above or even one of the above, but something happened to this man which has led him down a path of destruction, both to himself and others. The Bible tells us: *That which has been is what will be, That which is done is what will be done, And there is nothing new under the sun. Is there anything of which it may be said, "See, this is new?" It has already been in ancient times before us.* (Ecclesiastes 1:9-10)

I have had the awesome opportunities to speak to tens of thousands of young people. Over 2,000 years ago, we find this man cutting himself. Today, there are thousands of boys and girls who are cutting themselves. It is not something that is easily explained. Self-mutilation is not from above. It is something used by the devil in the lives of those who are hurting. And just as much as the thief comes to steal, kill and destroy, Jesus comes that we may have life and life more abundantly. (John 10:10)

But things are about to take on a drastic change for this man. When the townspeople show up, they find a man who had been transformed by the power of Jesus. He is at peace. He is seated instead of running all over the place. And he was in his right mind. Before we go further, there are some other things that the Bible doesn't tell us.

1. What does Jesus say to the man once the demons are expelled?
2. What is it like to have eye to eye contact with Jesus and see nothing but love?
3. What is it like to be touched by hands that were trying to change him rather than chain him?
4. What might it have been like to hear words like "I understand" or "I know what you've been through."
5. What is it like to hear a voice of compassion and understanding rather than one of fear and anger?
6. What is it like to feel like this may be the beginning of a new start?
7. What if Jesus hugged him? Wow!

The Bible doesn't tell us. Maybe it is not for us to know.

Maybe it is for us to put ourselves in this man's place and imagine what we would have liked or needed for Jesus to say to us in a moment like this. That man knows what Jesus did and said. The disciples know what Jesus did and said. And for this story, that is all that matters.

Regardless of what Jesus has done, the townspeople are afraid. They are no longer afraid of the man from the cemetery, but they are afraid of Jesus. They were afraid of the Prince of Peace. They were afraid of the Life Giver. They were afraid of the one who created them. They were afraid of the one they did not recognize.

The Bible says, *He was in the world and world was made through Him, and the world did not know Him. He came to His own and His own did not receive Him. But as many as received Him, to them He gave the right to become the children of God, to those who believe in His name.* (John 1:10-12)

As a result, the townspeople begin to plead with Jesus to leave. One thing I have learned about the Lord, He will never force Himself on you. Jesus did one other thing. He introduced Himself to the man. He did not need or want a demon to do it for Him. Did you notice the last part of verse 12?

It says, "To those who believe in His name." The only one who is not asking Jesus to leave is the man whose life has been radically changed by Jesus. I believe at this point, he too has become a child of God.

As Jesus and the disciples began to get into the boat, the man wants to go with Jesus. Maybe his attitude is: if they don't want Him, I don't need them. We don't know. That's just my imagination. What Jesus says to him has become one of my favorite scriptures in the Bible. *"Go home to your own people," he told him, "And tell them what the Lord has done for you, and how kind He has been to you."* Mark 5:19 (Phillips Translation).

Never once in this story is Jesus angry with this man. Never does He yell at him for getting himself in league with the demons. Never once does He rebuke the wayward behavior. He simply blesses him beyond his wildest imagination. He stops the storm that is raging in his life and its effects. He sends him home a new person.

The man lives in a city called Decapolis. He gets home and begins to publish all that Jesus had done in his life. I am sure that he takes no credit for himself. The Bible tells us in the book of Matthew, that when Jesus returned, those people bring out all those who were sick and demon possessed and He healed them all. I have to believe that some of that is because of this man's testimony.

Jesus gives us a testimony. Will we allow Him into our lives to heal or expel what ails us? Will we allow him to take charge of the storms that we can't handle? Will we go to the Lord about our behaviors and attitudes that we know don't come from Him? Will we take ownership for the issues that are ours and simply cast them at His feet?

Lord, heal the wounds of our lives. Enable us to forgive those who have hurt us. Enable us to forgive ourselves for those we have hurt.

Enable us to forgive ourselves for the self-inflicted wounds of our lives. Enable us to stop looking over our shoulders to things of the past that we have done or have been done to us. Lastly, Jesus, may we find ourselves sitting at your feet and listening to what you have to say in your Word. Heal us, Jesus, we ask. There is nothing impossible with You.

You have but to speak, and it can be done. There is no storm that You, Lord, cannot handle.

## Chapter 14

# *Hope in Frustration*

*"Casting all your care upon him; for he cares for you."* 1 Peter 5:7

Have you ever been frustrated? Have you ever reached your wit's end?

Have you tried everything you could think of and nothing seems to work? Have you become so frustrated that you decide to throw in the towel?

How many times have you looked in the mirror and did not like what you saw?

Maybe there were bulges on your body where at one time or another there were none. You say to yourself, "Enough is enough." You decide to go to the gym. You decide to go on a diet. It starts out great for a day or two, or maybe even a week or more.

Then, all of a sudden you find yourself right back where you started. Those same eating habits return.

You come up with every excuse imaginable about why you haven't been to the gym. You take another look in the mirror and those bulges have not moved. As a matter of fact, there might even be a few more. You walk away with your tail between your legs and your head hung low. You enter what I call, "The Valley of Frustration." I'm sure that most if not all of us have dealt with one or more issues in life that we just couldn't seem to control by our own strength.

I have been to that valley so many times. Once in a while, you hear a commercial on television or radio. The person in the commercial speaks with such hope and excitement. They give great assurance about the results of this "miracle cure." It can do things like no other. For a minimal fee, it can be yours. Could this be it? Is this what I have missed all along? You take down the phone number or the web address and you order the product. And you are off to the races.

In a couple of days, it arrives. You carefully do what the directions say and you wait for your miracle. Unfortunately, the miracle doesn't come. Nothing seems to change. You find yourself back in the Valley.

The Valley Experience isn't just limited to weight loss. It can be found in many of life's challenges. You make so many promises that you lose track. You promise not to scream at the kids. You tell your wife you will not say condescending things to her anymore. You promise not to lose your temper.

Maybe you promise that you will not look at pornography ever again or participate in some of the behavior that it leads to.

You promise that you will give up drinking because of the addiction that snares you. But the feeling arises and you listen to that inner voice that has spoken to you so many times before.

You have smooth sailing for a few days or even a few weeks, only to find yourself trapped again in its cruel claws. You take the tumble and frustration and discouragement sets in.

It could be ANY number of setbacks. It could be the inability to catch up with your bills, or the loss of your job, or the waywardness of one of your kids to the point that you don't know what to do with him or her -- or yourself for that matter. As you read this, what is one thing that strikes you as to what leads to your Valley?

One thing is for sure; nothing seems to change. You find yourself in that Valley again. While the Lord should be the first place we turn for help, often, He is our last resort. He is the last place where we REALLY can get help. Amazingly and thankfully, He is willing to respond. We are reminded that when we are not faithful, He is faithful still. He cannot deny Who He is (2 Timothy 2:13).

That is how it is for the person in the next scripture account. Her story can be found in Mark 5:21-34. Jesus and his disciples arrive on the shore. A great multitude gathers to meet Him. By now, He has done so much and healed so many. People want to be near Him. Some need a miracle. Some need healing. Some just need a word of encouragement. Remember, *"No man ever spoke like this Man."* (John 7:46)

First, however, there is an account of another man in the crowd. He is not just any man. The man's name is Jairus. He is the ruler of the synagogue. He is responsible for the spiritual and business matters of the synagogue. He would be the equivalent of a pastor of a local church.

As a public figure, nearly everyone in the crowd would have recognized Him. Maybe some are wondering why He is there on that day. Maybe some are thinking, "Surely he can't be here to see Jesus." Most of the religious leaders have rejected Jesus as anyone who could be the savior of the world. At that time, they hated him and were plotting to have him killed.

On this day, Jairus has an urgent need. It is not for himself. It's a need for someone that he loves, maybe more than anyone -- his 12-year-old daughter. She is sick and near the point of death. Jairus has probably gone to the doctors of the town and gotten no positive results. He is at his wit's end. Undoubtedly, he has heard about Jesus. He has heard that he casts out demons and heals the sick. Could this possibly be the miracle that he has been looking for?

Maybe he says to himself, "What have I got to lose? My prayers don't seem to be working." He reasons within himself and decides, "I am going to this Man. Maybe He will come and heal my little girl." He finds himself with the multitude waiting for Jesus. When Jesus disembarks from the boat, Jairus comes and falls at His feet. If any of Jairus' religious colleagues would have seen this, it might have been reason for him to lose his position in the synagogue.

But on this day, Jairus doesn't care. His love for his child overrides his care about what anyone might think. He tells Jesus the grim details of his daughter's impending death. He asks, no, begs Jesus to come to his home and heal her (though he doesn't have to). Immediately, Jesus senses the need and takes off to Jairus' house. His disciples and the crowd that had gathered follow Him.

Have you ever prayed for God to move on your behalf? Have you ever reached out to Him and heaven seemed quiet that day? Have you ever prayed for someone and saw God answer that prayer, but now when you're in need, He seems nowhere to be found? If you have ever read this story, and even if not, I wonder: What is going through Jairus' mind as they walk towards his house?

Maybe he thinks, "I hope He's all that I have heard that He is."

Or maybe, "I hope I haven't put my eggs in the wrong basket."

Or, "I hope God isn't angry with me because I have turned to this man."

Lastly, "I hope none of my religious buddies hear about this."

Jairus is not the only one with a need in the crowd. There is a woman who has a hemorrhage. She has been bleeding for 12 years. As a matter of fact, she has been bleeding for as long as Jairus' daughter has been on this earth. The scriptures tell us that she too wants to be cured of this malady.

She has gone from doctor to doctor and instead of getting better, she has only gotten worse. The only thing that doctors have done for her is take her money (Mark 5:26-27).

To make matters worse, because of her illness, Jewish law deems that she is ceremonially unclean. Fortunately, she too has heard about Jesus. She has tried everything that medicine could offer, and there has been no change. Maybe she reasons within herself, "What do I have to lose?"

According to the scriptures, she says to herself, *If only I can touch His clothes, I shall be made well.* (Mark 5:28)

Maybe she also says, "I hope I am not wasting my time again. At least this time, it's free."

She works her way through the crowd. She's tired. She's weary. She's anemic. However, there is a glimmer of hope flickering deep down in her heart. I believe that even as she approaches Jesus from behind him, He knows she's coming.

In a lunge of desperation, she reaches out and touches the hem of Jesus' garment. As she does so, she feels a surge of power enter into her body. Immediately, she realizes that she is healed. Jesus also knows that His power (virtue) has gone out of Him. He turned around to see who had done this. He asks, "Who touched me?" Mark 5:30. In the Luke 8 account, they all denied touching Him. Peter replies, *Master, the multitudes throng and press you and you say, 'Who touched me?'* (Luke 8:45)

Jesus scans the crowd. Maybe just for a moment, His eyes look into hers. Verse 47 says, *Fearing and trembling, knowing what has happened to her, she came and fell down before Him and told Him the whole truth.* (Luke 8:47)

To me, this is the amazing part of the story. I wonder what Jairus is doing or saying to himself as Jesus listens to her whole story. Maybe he has thoughts such as, "Did He forget my daughter is dying?" "Doesn't He realize my daughter's situation is much worse than hers?" Or, "Hey, I was first in the line!" Finally, Jesus finishes with the woman. He sends her on her way with these words: *Daughter, be of good cheer, your faith has made you well.* (Luke 8:48)

She is able to pursue life and live to the fullest. She no longer has the stigma of being unclean. No more empty promises from doctors who promise relief only to relieve her of her money. The power of God has been demonstrated in her life. She will never be the same again. She cast her care upon Jesus, and she was not disappointed.

Jairus too is relieved, thinking "now we can get to the real important matter, my daughter." The Bible doesn't say he felt that way, but he may have. I might have felt that way too if one of my children or grandchildren was dying, and when I needed Jesus, He stopped to heal someone else first.

As they turned to the road, Jairus' servants arrive with disturbing news. I have found out that in life, there is no shortages in messengers who bring bad news. (Mark 5:35) (Also read Job 1:13-19). The messengers tell Jairus, "Your daughter is dead. Why trouble the Teacher any further?"

I can only imagine the trap door of Jairus' heart springing open and for a moment, leaving him to fall into an abyss.

Thank God that Jesus is so much more than a teacher, and Jairus will soon find this out. Jesus immediately turns to Jairus and says, "Do not be afraid, only believe." (Mark 5:36). These words would be ludicrous if the one who was saying them was not Jesus. I think the words were reminding Jairus to maintain the faith that he had in Him on the shore. Maybe Jairus says to himself, "Okay. I have come this far. I won't give up now." Jesus continues on to Jairus' house with those who are following.

Upon their arrival, there is a tumult of people weeping and wailing loudly. Jesus confronts their noise with a question and statement, "Why make this commotion and weep? The child is not dead, but sleeping." (Mark 5:39)

Then, they go from weeping to ridiculing Jesus. That makes me wonder how serious their weeping is. But there is no doubt that the girl is dead. However, as soon as Jesus speaks those powerful words that she was only asleep, life immediately comes back into that child!

Then, Jesus sends everyone away and goes into the house where the child is lying. He is accompanied by Jairus, his wife, James, John and Peter. He takes the little girl by the hand, and said to her "Talitha, cumi," which is translated, "Little girl I say to you arise." (Mark 5:41)

The Bible says the parents are completely astonished. One author wrote about this and said, "The joy of her parents knew no bounds." I like that.

Cheeks that had gone pale are now beginning to flush with color as her blood begins to recirculate in her body and her spirit returns to her.

It has been a roller coaster of a day. A day of frustration and fear is turned into a day of joy and excitement in a new-found faith. A day when two people dare to stop being frustrated and decide to put their eggs in one basket. They cast all of their care upon Jesus and find out that He really does care for them.

I would hope that we won't stay frustrated too long. I pray that when challenges confront us, we would turn to Jesus sooner than later. I pray that we would not waste time seeking other solutions first and then turn to Him as a last resort. I pray that we would know that when all else fails, Jesus has the ability to come through as He has promised. It is not feeling that God cares for us that matters, it is KNOWING that He cares. That is the issue. And that is our hope!

# "For We Are Saved By Hope"

## Chapter 15

# *Hope in All This*

*"We should like you, our brothers, to know something of what we went through in Asia. At that time we were completely overwhelmed, the burden was more than we could bear, in fact we told ourselves that this was the end. Yet we believe now that we had this experience of coming to the end of our tether that we might learn to trust, not in ourselves, but in God who can raise the dead. It was God who preserved us from imminent death, and it is he who still preserves us. Further, we trust him to keep us safe in the future, and here you can join in and help by praying for us, so that the good that is done to us in answer to many prayers will mean eventually that many will thank God for our preservation."* II Corinthians 1:8 (Phillips NT) II Corinthians 2:8-11 (Phillips Translation)

I love the above verse, especially the way that it is explained in this particular translation. It is from a letter written by the Apostle Paul. Let's just take a look at it in simplistic terms. He is sharing with the church of Corinth regarding an ordeal he went through while he was in Asia.

He is looking at something that happened to him in retrospect. It is an opportunity to look at something that happened in his past. It would be similar to driving your car through something and looking in the rearview mirror. The danger is past and maybe you are astonished that you made it through.

As far as Paul is concerned, whatever happened was so overwhelming that he felt that it was more than he could bear. Even though it is Paul who wrote that the Lord will never allow us to be tempted above that which we would be able to stand and in the temptation (or test), He will provide the way of escape that we could bear it (1 Corinthians 10:13), that verse did not seem to matter in this situation.

Have you ever been overwhelmed? Have you ever been in a situation and was unable to see the hand of God? Regardless of what we don't see, we have to know that the Lord is faithful and He has a plan. It seems to me that God is always up to something, as He was in this situation.

Paul states that the burden was more than he could bear. However, he must have been able to bear it or the above verse would have never been written. It wasn't only Paul who felt this way but some of his companions did as well. He says, "We told ourselves that this was the end."

But now, in retrospect and understanding, they NOW see what God was up to. Often when we go through something, we do not easily see the hand of God or know His plans. That is when we have to use the measure of faith that has been given to us (Romans 12:3).

It seems to me that Paul and his friends had given up hope during the time of the ordeal. Maybe that hope was restored when they looked back over their shoulders and it was THEN plain to see what the Lord was doing. God was bringing his followers to the end of themselves that they might 'learn not to trust in themselves, but in God who could raise the dead." Wow!!!

Paul had to learn not to trust in himself. To me, this means that to a certain extent, he WAS trusting in himself. Wow! This is the man who wrote 13 books in the Bible. He had to learn. If Paul the Apostle had to learn, how much do I have yet to learn? This is the man that was caught up into the third heaven. This is the man who had a personal encounter with Jesus on the Road to Damascus. This is the man who preached the Gospel to the Jews, Gentiles, and Kings.

Paul had to learn a lesson. If he had to learn a lesson, then I am in good company as I learn the lessons of life. I learn a lesson each time the Lord puts His hand to the plow regarding the good work He has begun in me. God wants me to learn the lessons that He is teaching. For the Believer, what could be more important than learning to trust God? For it is the Lord who says, *You will keep him/ her in perfect peace whose mind is stayed on Me, because they Trust Me.* (Isaiah 26:3)

For me, my journey has been a litany of learning lessons: the good, the bad, and the ugly. Yet through it all, the Lord is asking me to trust Him. If I want His peace (His perfect peace), I must be willing to trust Him. It doesn't always feel good. It doesn't always seem good.

The only thing I can say is if I trust God and what He has given us in His Word, things have a way of working out for my good (Romans 8:28).

As I look back over the years, I can see the good, the bad, and the ugly. When I look at the good, I already know what to do with that: appreciate it and learn from it. Be thankful for all the people that God has placed in my life to love me and care for me, speak truth and encouragement into my life. Most of all, to be thankful for those instances of grace when you know the Lord intervened in some significant way. This book would have never been written had He not intervened in those instances.

But what about the bad and the ugly? What about the wounds that have been inflicted over the years: wounds that were inflicted by others and way too often, self-inflicted?

It has taken me so long to learn that I cannot change anything that has happened to me in the past. I cannot go back and undo anything that I have done. I cannot pretend that the things that happened to me at the hands of others didn't happen. The one thing I can do is hopefully and prayerfully learn from those things. That is something that is easier said than done. But it is not impossible with the help of the Lord. A bigger question is: what does the Lord do with those things?

His word gives some great insights to what He does. First of all, in Romans 8:28, He says He is able to work everything for the good to those who love Him and are called according to His purpose.

He doesn't say that everything is good. He says He can work it together for good to those who love Him and are called according to His purpose. If that is true (and I believe that it is, because His word says so), regardless of how bad and ugly a situation may have been, He is doing something good with it. That verse says, "to those who love Him, to those who are called according to His purpose." Maybe that means that my situation won't only work for my good, but also for the good of the others who are called according to His purpose. I even wonder if in working it together for my good, might there be an overflow into the lives of those who don't yet love Him.

Let me explain. When I went to Children's Village, I did not know the baggage that I was bringing with me. It did not take long for the Lord to start working and revealing that baggage.

I began to see myself in the lives of the kids I was "called" to minister to. I could relate to their pain and their anger.

As they began to trust me, they let me into deeper parts of their lives. As I allowed the Lord to heal me of my family baggage (which at first, I did not realize was there), He then allowed me to speak into their lives. I was able to speak with compassion and understanding.

I did not have to get "hooked" by their behaviors. When I say "hooked," I mean I did not have to internalize their brokenness. In other words, I did not have to let their issues become my issues.

I was able to see them with an understanding of what they were going through, because I had been through many of those things as well. I was able to empathize with them.

At that point, I did not even know what the Bible said on this issue. Here is what it says in II Corinthians 1:3-7; II Corinthians 1:3 (Phillips NT)

*"Thank God, the Father of our Lord Jesus Christ, that he is our Father and the source of all mercy and comfort. For he gives us comfort in our trials so that we in turn may be able to give the same sort of strong sympathy to others in theirs. Indeed, experience shows that the more we share Christ's suffering the more we are able to give of his encouragement. This means that if we experience trouble we can pass on to you comfort and spiritual help; for if we ourselves have been comforted we know how to encourage you to endure patiently the same sort of troubles that we have ourselves endured. We are quite confident that if you have to suffer troubles as we have done, then, like us, you will find the comfort and encouragement of God."*

Upon reading these verses, I could see God's plan at work in my life. I had never heard the word dysfunctional until I was an adult. However, in looking back, I can see that I came out of a dysfunctional family system. I find it amazing that in the last 25 years, the Lord has allowed me to go all over the world and speak to what seems like the most broken generation of kids the world has ever seen. Kids who come out of homes of fatherlessness, abuse, abandonment, rejection and sexual violation, families sent hither and yon, and a host of other issues.

Then, it is not only those kids, but folks in the church, who too have come to Christ just as they were. Just like the kids, they carry a host of hurts and wounds, some of which were other-inflicted and others self-inflicted. One thing I have learned about other-inflicted wounds and self-inflicted wounds, they are both painful and need to be healed. Max Lucado is quoted as saying, *"God loves you just the way you are, but He refuses to leave you that way. He wants you to be just like Jesus."*

A church that has a host of damaged people will only damage themselves and others. There must be the willingness to take a look at ourselves, open ourselves up to Jesus, and allow Him to touch that place of hurt. In my time of ministry, I have talked to a host of people who say, "But Bill, you don't understand." or they say, "You don't know all that I have been through."

I agree to some degree, but we do have a God who does understand. We have a God in the person of Jesus who has been through it all. The scripture says, *For we do not have a High Priest who cannot sympathize with our weaknesses, but was in all points tempted as we are, yet without sin.* (Hebrews 4:15)

Better still, the Message Translation interprets the same verse this way: *"We don't have a priest who is out of touch with our reality. He's been through weakness and testing, experienced it all—all but the sin."*

There is nothing that we go through that Jesus is not familiar with. He was despised, rejected, dishonored, abused, abandoned, lied to, lied on and violated.

He was murdered and He experienced many more injustices. He even knows what it feels like when a Father turns His face from His own Son. There is nothing that I bring before Him that He can't relate to. He can quickly enter into our hurts and wounded-ness.

Remember, the Bible says, *Who has believed our report? And to whom has the arm of the LORD been revealed? For He shall grow up before Him as a tender plant, And as a root out of dry ground. He has no form or comeliness; And when we see Him, there is no beauty that we should desire Him. He is despised and rejected by men, A Man of sorrows and acquainted with grief. And we hid, as it were, our faces from Him; He was despised, and we did not esteem Him. Surely He has borne our griefs and carried our sorrows; Yet we esteemed Him stricken, Smitten by God, and afflicted. But He was wounded for our transgressions, He was bruised for our iniquities; The chastisement for our peace was upon Him, And by His stripes we are healed. All we like sheep have gone astray; We have turned, every one, to his own way; And the LORD has laid on Him the iniquity of us all. He was oppressed and He was afflicted, Yet He opened not His mouth; He was led as a lamb to the slaughter, and as a sheep before its shearers is silent, So He opened not His mouth. He was taken from prison and from judgment, and who will declare His generation? For He was cut off from the land of the living; For the transgressions of My people He was stricken. And they made His grave with the wicked-- But with the rich at His death, Because He had done no violence, nor was any deceit in His mouth. "* (Isaiah 53:1-9)

Who is this God that would allow this to happen to Himself for the benefit of His people? God has gone out of his way to secure our eternity along with our healing, our joy, our peace, and our deliverance. His love for us is not only demonstrated for us at the Cross, but in so many other ways in our lives. Because of He has forgiven us, we are now enabled to forgive others and ourselves.

*Let there be no more resentment, no more anger or temper, no more violent self-assertiveness, no more slander and no more malicious remarks, Be kind to each other, be understanding. Be as ready to forgive others as God for Christ's sake has forgiven you.* (Ephesians 4:31-32 Phillips NT)

It is hard to believe that the Lord desires to step into the lives of His children. He is such a "hands on" God. He knows exactly where we stand and exactly what we need. After all, He is the God of ALL comfort and mercy.

There is a statement that goes around (mostly in the men's circles). It says, "It ain't about me!" It usually comes when someone does something for the Lord, and people want to give that person the credit. It sounds good and is good to an extent. However, when someone allows their Son to die for you, that person has made it all about you.

In the economy of God, it really is all about you and me (and He is the only one who can say that).

# *"For We Are Saved By Hope"*

## Chapter 16

# Hope in Ministry
# and Misery

*"Simon, Simon, Satan has asked to sift all of you as wheat. But I have prayed for you, Simon, that your faith may not fail. And when you have turned back, strengthen your brothers. But he replied, Lord, I am ready to go with you to prison and to death. Jesus answered, I tell you, Peter, before the rooster crows today, you will deny three times that you know me."* Luke 22:31-34 (NIV)

What an incredible moment for the disciples on the night that Jesus would be betrayed by one of them. It sounds like he is only speaking to Peter. However, in the original language, the first "you" is plural. Therefore, though focused on Peter, He is really speaking to all of them (I believe that it transcends down to you and me as well). He lets them know that He prays for them. They have seen the results of His prayers.

The second "you" is singular for *He ever lives to make intercession for us.* (Hebrews 7:25) Jesus even tells His disciples what He has prayed for them, "faith." Faith, without it, *"It is impossible to please the Lord".* (Hebrews 11:6)

He listens to the misguided zeal of one of his key disciples, Peter. Peter is a man who has over-estimated his own prowess. Jesus gives him an ominous prophecy. It is a prophecy that is too soon shrugged off by Peter.

So many things happen in those four verses. However, they are very important things to remember as we walk out our lives in Christ. To a minister of the Gospel, they should take on even more significant meaning and importance. *"For to whom much is given, much is required."* (Luke 12:48) I say this because the men that Jesus is addressing that night will all be ministers of the Gospel. We must remember that all scripture is "God breathed." (2 Timothy 3:16; NIV). When God gave us the word of God, it was for our benefit and edification.

The scriptures remind us that there wouldn't be enough books in the world to write down "all" the things that Jesus did. (John 21:25). That being said, why did God give us what He gave us? It would seem to me that the Gospels contain not only the God breathed things we would need, but also the handpicked things He wanted us to know. In those four short books as well as the rest of the Bible are written the words that will produce faith in our lives as well as instruct us on how to live our lives. I believe we are NOT to take the word of God for granted.

Man lives *"by every word that proceeds from the mouth of God"*. (Matthew 4:4) If I want to live, I need to pay close attention to what God has to say on a matter. When I began my Christian walk, I did just that, though I needed to learn what God was *really* saying. The word of God became important to me. I poured myself into the scriptures. I spent time in the presence of God in prayer. I hung out with other believers. I had a strong desire to walk in the Spirit.

I told anyone that I could get my hands on the Good News of the Kingdom. I was falling in love with the God who was in love with me. I cannot remember sin being too much of an issue for me and that might have been a bigger issue right there. The abundant life I had encountered was utterly amazing.

In those early days, God did amazing things in answer to my prayers. I prayed for situations (even parking spaces) and things would happen. I would pray for people, and the Lord would move in their behalf. If I saw something in the Bible, I felt that I could apply it to my life. I would go to God and remind Him that He was not a respecter of persons and ask Him to do the same thing for me. Often, He would do just that.

To a certain degree, I had become like a little child entering into the Kingdom of God (Matthew 18:3). However, at that time I did not know that much of what I was doing was legalism. I was living by the law. I was keeping most of the rules because the Bible said so. I was not living a life in response to what God had done for me, but in what I could do for Him. I was exhausting myself.

Slowly but surely, I was drifting. However, at the time, I did not know it. I was saying and doing a lot of things that were pushing people away more than drawing them to Jesus.

At this point, I want to make something very clear. Jesus said, *I come that you would have life and have it more abundantly.* (John 10:10) I thought that I was having life and having it more abundantly, and to a certain degree I was. However, looking back I can now see that a lot of it was not the abundance that Jesus was talking about when He said those words. It was a life greater than anything I had yet experienced, but little did I know it was nothing compared to what He had in store for me.

Often, if you watch the rerun of a movie, you see things that you missed the first time. There are many movies that I watch over and over. I enjoy them so much that I memorize the lines. If the beginning of my walk with Christ were a movie, I can now see so many of the things I missed the first time. I would not use that movie as a thing of enjoyment, but I would use it as a teaching tool "of things never to do again."

Of course, there would be things in the movie that I would do again, just not everything. One thing I would do is to receive Jesus. Since that moment, things have never been the same! The biggest lesson that I would have learned from the movie is: the process of finding out that how much God loves me is way more important than how much I love Him.

In regards to love, I would like to share a thought. Jesus said, *If you love Me, keep my commandments.* (John 14:15) The NIV says, *Anyone who loves me will obey my commands.*

The Message translation says, *If you love me, keep my commands.* I believe that it would be right to assume that obedience to what Jesus commands would be an evidence of our love for Him. If that is true, would our disobedience be an evidence of something else? At the very least, it might mean that we do not love Him as much as we say or think we do.

I truly believe that God cannot love me more than He does right now. I also believe that He will never love me any less. Of course, I have not always believed that. However, my love is not like His love. My love is fickle. My love goes up and down. His love is at full capacity all the time. I have love, He is love. Just like Peter, I have found that I do not love the Lord nearly as much as I think I do. And He loves me more than I can ever imagine.

Paul the apostle says, *For I am not ashamed of the Gospel of Christ, for it is the power of God to salvation for everyone who believes, for the Jew first and also for the Gentiles.* (Romans 1:16) Bill Paige is not ashamed of the Gospel of Christ either, but I am very much ashamed of some of my behavior in the last 36 years.

I look back at my disobedience. I look back at how many times I have grieved the Holy Spirit. I look at the hypocrisy that was in my life. I look at the times I encouraged people to turn away from the very things that I was involved in. At one point, I asked the Lord, "How could I have done those things?" This is the answer I believe I received from Him: "What difference does it make? Don't do them again."

Just like He told the woman in John 8, *Go and sin no more.* (John 8:11) He did not lecture her. He did not berate her. He commanded her, "Go and sin no more." I think He expected her to learn a great lesson of the grace of God, let the undeserved love she received that day to be a catalyst, and live her life responding to that love.

If Jesus commands us to do something, then based on John 15:5, He has to enable us to do it. For it is He who says, *Without Me, you can do nothing.* We are commanded to do exactly that in II Corinthians 5:14-15. Those verses read in the Phillips Translation*: We look at it like this: if one died for all men then, in a sense all men died, and His purpose in dying for them is that their lives should now be no longer lived for themselves but for Him who rose from the dead.*

At the time of this writing, I have been "following" Jesus for 36 years. That is quite a long time. During that time, there has been a lot of "sin and weight" that I did not lay aside. I don't feel that is necessary to go into all of the gory details. Just know there have been times of gross disobedience. There have been times of arrogant, critical, and judgmental displays of an attitude that is nothing like that of Jesus.

I have stepped over relational boundaries. I have finger-pointed at those who were guilty of the same sins that I had or was committing. I have had struggles with pornography that I needed counseling and prayer to be set free from. I have carried a multitude of baggage from my childhood that caused behavioral attitudes that were not in alignment with the Holy Spirit.

I have despised folks who chose an alternative lifestyle to the one I believed God had chosen for them. But unlike Jesus, I chose to judge them rather than love them. I have been both the prodigal son and the self-righteous brother (both of whom had to be contended with by the Father).

I have loved what I was doing for God more than I have loved God. I have been guilty of trying to do things to get God to love me rather that bask in the love He had already bestowed upon me. I have at times failed to love my neighbor as myself. When I look at the story labeled, "The Young Rich Ruler," found in Mark 10, I have found myself to be guilty of all the commandments that Jesus mentions.

Maybe you are now saying, "Even murder?" God says in His word that if you hate someone in your heart, it is the same as murder. (1 John 3:15) With that established, yes, even murder. By the way, the word of God also says, *For whosoever shall keep the whole law, and yet offend in one point, he is guilty of all.* (James 2:10) In other words, I have been a mess. It is only by God's faithfulness, goodness, graciousness, forgiveness, patience, forbearance, and love that I am standing today.

My life was miserable during the times that I was away from "Home" – away from His presence. Yet the Lord sustained me. He never kicked me to the curb. During these times of failure, God would allow, "this far but no further." Not for one moment did I ever feel that God was condoning behavior that was not in alignment with His will. But not once did I feel that He had walked away from me. I felt that He should have, but He didn't. I was like a man caught in a revolving door. I did not know what to do.

I have found that no sooner do I forget the demonstration of God's love at Calvary, than I am as good as gone. The moment I forget grace, mercy, and goodness found in His love, I am as good as gone. The moment that I forget that the God of the universe has gone out of His way to choose me for His family and Kingdom, I am a dead man. And in knowing this, there have been so many times I have done just that -- "forgotten." Though I really have not forgotten, I just have put all of that on the back burner of my heart and lived life for myself.

In Hebrews 12, we are told to look to Jesus, the author and finisher of our faith, who for the joy that was set before Him, He endured the Cross. Now He is seated at the right hand of the throne of God (Hebrews 12:1-3). I have thought often of the joy. What could it be? I think it could be pleasing the Father by doing His will. Secondly, maybe, He looked up the corridor of time and saw us (humanity without hope) and said, "They're worth it!"

I was at a conference for Young Life staff when the movie, *The Passion of the Christ* was released. We were allowed to see it before it hit the movie screens in the country. I remember walking in and there were boxes of tissues at every row of seats. There were about 4,000 of us, so there were rows and rows of seats.

I looked at the boxes and scoffed to myself. I thought, "That is a little overkill, don't you think?" Before that movie ended, I could have used an entire box by myself. I cried like a baby. Snot was running out of my nose. Whoever I was sitting next to was trying to console me.

I was a mess. I saw on the screen this story that I had told to untold thousands of kids and adults.

It came to life. It hit me right between the eyes: "He did that for me." It was no longer for them; it was for me! I did not know what to do with the emotions that were running through my mind. However, God turned the light on that day in a way that He had never turned it on before. The moment was more powerful than the day that I gave my heart to Christ, more importantly, the day He gave His heart to me. It was all about me.

There is a phrase, "It's not about me." People sometimes use it when they don't want to take any of God's glory. That is rightfully so. However, when God lets His Son die on a cross for you, in His economy, He has made it all about you. I strongly believe that is one thing He never wants you to put on the back burner! Yet we do it.

That being said, it is the goodness of the Lord that has brought me home. Like the prodigal son, if there was one thing he knew, it was that he could go home. He probably knew His father loved him, but like me, he had no idea how much his father loved him. He had found out the hard way, just like I did, that God's word is true.

The Bible says, *"The way of a transgressor is hard."* (Proverbs 13:15) It is always going to be hard when you make up your mind to do it your way. If only you could hear the voice of God in the Spirit world when He says, "How's that working for you?"

If the seed of God is planted in you, I believe you will never be satisfied with sin. Yes, you can commit it, but it will never truly satisfy you. The Spirit of God is there. He is prodding you to come home. He will never force you to come home (though He could), but by His loving kindness, He has chosen to draw you back to His side. (Jeremiah 31:3)

How many lessons have to be learned before, like the prodigal son, we come to our senses? Or maybe after we come to our senses, we go home only to be tantalized to leave home again. Do we truly have to be the dog that returns to his vomit (Proverbs 26:11) to find out that vomit is not really the best thing on the menu?

Yet, God has been faithful. He has promised in His word, that when we are faithless, He will be faithful still because He cannot deny Himself (II Timothy 2:13). He has promised that the One who has begun a good work in us will perform it, even until the day of Jesus Christ (Philippians 1:6). The investment the Father has made in us cost Him a lot. It cost the life of His Son, Jesus. At times, I have been awestruck by the goodness of God. The foolish question is, "Why?" It is a question that will probably never be answered fully until we stand before Him, face to face.

I have found out that life outside of His will is really not life at all. It is misery. Misery because I have chosen to live my life in a way that is not designed for me. If you went fishing and caught a fish, took it off the hook, and laid it on the ground, it would flap around and gasp for air. If you could talk to the fish and ask what it wanted, what would it say?

"Put me back into the water!" It would say that because it is designed to live in the water, not on the land.

If you were to ask the fish, "How are you feeling?" I think one answer could be, "Miserable." I believe it is similar for the Believer. We can get along for a while in sin, but if Christ is really in your life, sin makes life miserable. We were created in Him to do "good works" (Ephesians 2:10). Nothing else will truly work. Jesus Himself did not go around not committing sin (though He never did). The Bible says, *How God anointed Jesus of Nazareth with the Holy Spirit and with power, who went about doing good and healing all who were oppressed by the devil, for God was with Him.* (Acts 10:38) He was consumed with doing good, therefore He never did wrong. He was good conscious and we as humans are sin conscious. He was consumed with doing the right thing, and we get caught up with not doing the wrong thing. At least I do.

However, when I am consumed with loving God and living my life in ways that reflects that, I am at peace. When I get focused on His love for me rather than my love for Him, I am a happy camper. When I (through the help of the Holy Spirit) love my neighbor as myself, life is so much sweeter. Anything short of that is misery.

I have played a game in which the adults put something in one of their hands. It might be a piece of candy or some money. They enclose it in their fist. Then they extend it to a child and say, "Which hand has the prize in it?"

The child makes a choice and the person opens that hand. If it is the right hand, they give the child its contents.

Usually, if the child chooses wrong, they get the prize anyway. I love the verse that says, *I call heaven and earth as witnesses today against you, that I have set before you, life and death, blessing and cursing: therefore choose life and live, that both you and your descendants may live:* (Deuteronomy 30:19)

God sets four choices before Israel. Two are good and two are not. Rather than wait for them to make the wrong choice, He tells them what to choose. He says, "Choose life that both you and your descendants may live." He doesn't want them to make a wrong choice. And the choice they make will both impact the chooser and their descendants. When Jesus shows up on the earth, He says of Himself, *I am the way, the truth, and the life.* (John 14:6) The scriptures tell us to *"Choose today who you will serve."* (Joshua 24:15) If we choose "the life," it will have eternal blessings, not just for ourselves but our descendants as well. I believe any other choice will lead to misery, which God calls death and cursing.

I have written this chapter primarily for those who feel that they love Jesus. You love Him, yet your life (far more often than not) reflects a different story. You find yourself trudging through life with all of its ups and downs, and far more downs than ups.

You love God but you are in misery. You are in misery because of the continual failings. You are in misery because you wrongly think that God has turned His back on you. You are in misery because you have not kept all the promises you have made. You are in misery because of the consequences of poor choices.

I pray that you will be able to lift your head up. Please know this: Just as surely as your sin will find you out, God will find you out as well. He's looking for you. He came to seek and to save those who are lost. (Luke 19:10)

When you are found, He rejoices over you like the shepherd, the woman, and the Father in Luke 15. You might ask: "How can I be found?" STOP RUNNING! Call out to Him. Turn and start heading for home. One step at a time, but don't stop. He sees you from afar. Then He starts running -- not from you -- but to you.

Surprisingly, He will not give you what you deserve. He will smother you with kisses and gifts. If you don't believe me, read the story in Luke 15 again. This time, take your time. Listen to what God is truly trying to convey. Receive it, receive Him. *He came to His own, and His own did not receive Him. But as many as received Him, He gave the right to become the children of God, to those who believe in His name.* (John 1:11-12)

Today, by the grace of God, my hope is secure. I have chosen life. I am back home where I belong. I never want to leave again. I have had the opportunity to compare life and misery. Life is so much better.

CHOOSE LIFE AND THEN LIVE IT TO THE FULLEST!!

# "For We Are Saved By Hope"

## Chapter 17

# *Hope in Coming Home*

*"And not many days after the younger son gathered all together, and took his journey into a far country, and there wasted his substance in riotous living."* Luke 15:13

When I read the Bible, the stories turn into movies for me. This is because of the influence of writers like Phillip Yancey, Max Lucado, Brennan Manning, and most of all, Ken Gire. These men have helped to develop what I hope is a holy imagination.

The story labeled "The Prodigal Son" is said to be one of the most preached stories in the Bible. Like many others, I believe that it has been improperly labeled. Maybe, it should be called the "Loving Father." I know when, included with the preceding stories, it is a parable about the searching for lost things. But because it is in story form, for the purposes of this book, I will treat it like a story.

There would come a day in the life of the younger brother in Luke 15, that he would decide to leave the "ranch."

He goes to his father and says, "Give me the portion of good that falls to me." (Luke 15:12) Notice he says, he did not ask. Another way of looking at it would be: "I don't want to wait for you to die. Give me what I got coming. Now!!"

Can you imagine if God ever gave us "what we got coming?" Yet, He will often allow us to have what we want, even if it is not good for us. Many times, He will let us have what we want, if we demand it. Often, it will be to our dismay.

Have you ever wondered why the younger son left home? The Bible never tells us. I think the Lord leaves that up to our imaginations. Again, I know that it is a parable. Yet the Lord does not take away our ability to think about things. What is going on in his life that is drawing him away from the ranch? How has he become so disenchanted?

In the story, many believe the father represents God the Father. If that is the case, who would want to leave such a loving entity? The son's needs are being met. He has servants, food, a place to sleep, a roof over his head and we will learn in the story, that all the father had is his and his brother's. Yet, there is something drawing him to leave. And to leave with an attitude.

When I think of this story, I often wonder if the unloving, self-righteous brother was the cause. We don't find out about him until later in the story. Too often, that is the case when God's children end up leaving home for a faraway country. There is always a reason, but when it comes to our relationship with the Lord, there is never a good excuse for leaving.

In my lifetime, I have been on numerous journeys. Many of them were incredible and some of them were disasters. Again, having grown up in a dysfunctional family, I believe that I wanted to escape and go on a journey: ANYWHERE!! Unlike the young man in this story – who had everything anyone could ask for – my years as a youth were full of turmoil.

I was very discontented with what was taking place in my home. The abuse and lack of love from the person I thought was my mother -- but wasn't -- had become unbearable. The love of my earthly father was unquestionable. He had never said a mean-spirited word to me nor had he ever abused me. He was always there for me. He loved me unconditionally. He did not express a lot of verbal affirmation, but his presence was more than enough. He never did one thing that would justify my leaving. But my mind was made up. I had to go.

As a sidebar, the scriptures record another incident where Paul warns some folks about the possibility of a disastrous journey. No one listens to him. They get into the boat and set sail. In the Philips Translation of the Bible, it says, *So, when a moderate breeze sprang up, thinking they had obtained just what they wanted, they weighed anchor, and coasted along, hugging the shores of Crete. But before long a terrific gale, which they called a north-eastern, swept down of them from the land.* (Acts 27:13-14)

When they begin the journey, everything seems to be smooth sailing. Before long, all hell was breaking loose. Before long, the ship sinks and loses the cargo. By the grace of Almighty God, not a single life was lost.

However, as Sean Connery said in the movie, *The Untouchables*: "There ends the lesson." When all is said and done, there is always a lesson to be learned. The Lord will make sure that you and I learn it: on or off the ranch!

The circumstances of life will often bring us to our senses, though there are multitudes who refuse to learn. In Luke 15, the younger brother has come to the end of his rope. He is in a pigpen, desiring to eat the food the pigs eat. He comes to the end of his rope and then "he comes to his himself" (his senses) (Luke 15:17). A glimmer of hope has come alive within him. He simply takes a look at the options and says, "I am going home."

He knows he can go home. He knows his father loves him. He just doesn't know how much. Even in the midst of that, he was going home on his terms. Though they seem honorable, they are his thoughts. Remember, *For My thoughts are not your thoughts, nor are your ways My ways," says the Lord. For as the heavens are higher than the earth, so are My ways higher than your ways, and My thoughts higher than your thoughts.* (Isaiah 55:8-9)

Take a look at Luke 15:18-19 and hear the son's thoughts: *I will arise and go to my father, and will say to him, "Father I have sinned against heaven and before you, I am no longer worthy to be called your son. Make me like one of the hired servants."*

He starts off good by taking ownership for his behavior. He decides his worthiness (of which God can only determine).

Then, he starts telling (or recommending) what his father should do with him. Again, something that only the Father can do.

How does the father want to handle this situation? Let's take a look at Luke 15:20: *And he arose and came to his father. But when he was still a great way off, his father saw him and had compassion, and ran and fell on his neck and kissed him.* One translation says, "Smothered him with kisses."

The son then tells his father the lines that he has rehearsed over and over on the journey back home. By the way, I would think that journey seemed a lot longer than the journey when he departed. The response of the father is like no other. Hear what is recorded in Luke 15:22-24: *"But the father said to his servants, 'Bring out the best robe and put it on him, and put a ring on his hand and sandals on his feet. 'Bring the fatted calf here and kill it, and let us eat and be merry; 'for this my son was dead and is alive again; he was lost and is found. And they began to be merry."*

Wow! What kind of a father is this? I have often thought about this in regards to my life and even how I entreated my own sons during their times of waywardness. I was nothing like this father. This father even goes on to give this son a party with music and dancing. However, this father does not succumb to the wishes of his son. He does not allow him to go and live with the hired servants. This son would not have to work his way back to his father's love. He has his father's love. He would not determine his own worthiness.

The father's behavior demonstrates the realization of the son's worthiness. What an incredible scene.

As the hired servants watch this scene, I wonder how many of them wished that the father was their father. Jesus wants us to know the love of that Father. Because that Father is His Father.

There used to be a phrase in the hood, "Who's your Daddy?" I believe Jesus would say, "I hope and pray that My Daddy is your Daddy."

The story doesn't end there. The older brother returns from the field and becomes indignant when he hears and sees all that has taken place (Luke 15:25-32). He can't believe that the knucklehead has returned and to make matters worse, Dad has given him a pardon and a party. He refuses to join the festivities. The father goes out to entreat this older son, who at this time is just as wayward as his brother was in the far country. He is not in alignment with his father. He does not share the same views as his father. Like his younger brother, he too wants it his way. A classic "Burger King," commercial says, "Have it your way," but when it comes to the things of God, it just doesn't go that way.

I wonder why the older brother is not joyous over the return of his brother. I guess there are a lot of reasons, but none of them would be legitimate. I have often seen many people return from the "far country" in their walks with God. Instead of getting a hug and a kiss, they get a litany of questions. Instead of a party and celebration, they have to face an inquisition.

Did you notice that when the younger brother returns home, the father does not ask him one question? He is just elated to have him back at the ranch.

The older brother challenges his sibling's behavior and his father's attitude toward both of them. The father even has to remind the older brother of his kinship to his younger brother. The older brother has left the ranch without ever taking a step.

When Jesus tells this parable, he is speaking to two groups of people: the religious "right" and sinners. The religious right does not like the fact that Jesus hangs around sinners and would even dare to have meals with them. Can you imagine how those sinful people felt about how they were being treated? The looks of scorn and disdain, judgmental attitudes, and criticisms were probably more than one could bear. No wonder the knuckleheads did not want to come home. Who needs that?

I have been both the recipient and the dispenser of that kind of bad attitude. Early on in my walk with Christ, when I thought I had it all together, I was so critical, judgmental and arrogant. It was all couched in religion. A woman sent me a note one day that read, "I thank God that you don't have a hell to put someone in."

Shortly after that, I left "the ranch." I found myself in need of the love and grace that I refused to give to others. One day, I came home from a journey and got hugs and kisses from my Daddy!! Hopefully, I will never treat returnees the way I once did. Just as much, and maybe even more so, I pray that I won't leave the ranch anymore either.

I think that it is often why some people leave the church. Just as much, I believe this is why some people find it hard to return. Either way there is no excuse.

Our loving heavenly Father has done nothing to drive us away. Nor has He done anything to keep us away. It's just the opposite: He loves us unconditionally. He sees us in our wayward states and desires for us to come home. He desires for us to come to repentance. He has gone out of his way to prove it. *The Lord is not slack concerning his promise, as some count slackness; but is longsuffering to us-ward, not willing that any should perish, but that all should come to repentance.* (2 Peter 2:9) Did you see that little word that means so much: "all?" Who better to write that than Peter?

The last verse of Luke 15 says it all as far as God's way of looking at things. It says*: It was right that we should make merry and be glad, for your brother was dead and is alive again, and was lost and is found!* (Luke 15:32)

Again, I ask: what kind of a Daddy is this? He is Jesus' Daddy, and He says, "Bring your journey to an end and come home." He also says, "Don't worry about others in the family." He knows how to deal with them.

This is just between us and Daddy -- and only Daddy.

# About The Author

A gifted, passionate speaker, Bill Paige has brought a depth of life experiences including 20 years of police and detective work in and around the New York City metropolitan area to his audiences. He also served for 14 years as the associate chaplain at Children's Village, working with emotionally disturbed boys in the city. He recently retired from 15 plus years of senior leadership in Young Life, most recently as a Special Assistant to the President. An ordained minister, he is an Associate Pastor at Christian International Church in Lincoln Park, NJ.

Bill has held month-long assignments at Young Life camp properties where he has spoken to thousands of young people regarding the basics of the Christian faith. In addition, he has addressed chapel services for both the National Football League (NFL) and Major League Baseball (MLB) teams, including two opportunities to speak at the NFL Pro Bowl. He has appeared in talks at high school and college assemblies and traveled internationally to share the gospel of Jesus Christ.

*If you wish to order additional copies of
"Hope on a Rope", or look into scheduling
Bill Paige for a speaking engagement, you may
contact him directly at Bill Paige Ministries.
The email address is <u>BPaige10919@gmail.com</u>*